The E-Z
Home Inspection Guide

All Rights Reserved
Worldwide Copyright © 1993, 1994
Joseph A. Ellul Jr. and Bonnie D. Robinson
E & R Marketing • Lutz, FL 33549

Printed in the United States of America

Revised Edition

ISBN 0-9639584-9-6

Any reproduction of "The E-Z Home Inspection Guide" is prohibited in any form, parts or by any electronic or mechanical means. This is including information storage and retrieval systems, without written permission from the Authors.

Disclaimer: E & R Marketing, its Agents, Distributors and the Authors of "The E-Z Home Inspection Guide" do not assume any liability or responsibility for the user's actions. Use this guide safely, and at your own risk.

*In memory of our fathers
Joseph Ellul, Sr. and Henry Davis.
Thank you for your Love, Knowledge
and Everlasting Support*

ACKNOWLEDGMENTS

The Authors thank our families and friends for all of their loving support.

We express our sincere appreciation to our special friends in Michigan, Texas and Florida for their inspiration and all the time they allowed to review and analyze our Guide.

Bryant Gardner, Vince & Anita Powierski, Joseph Cusenza, Paul Sowerby, Richard & Trina Woelfel, Steve & Tisha Moore, Harvey & Catherine Van Buhler, Ann & Jerry Jones, Luke & Pierre St. Pierre, Tim Watters, Hugh McCombs, William Hanlon, Joe & Diane Johnson, Geno Korytko, Lynn Arnett, Ross Knighton
Also
Lon & Barbara Grossman for their "Maintenance Schedule" and George M. Johnson for his "Information Form" used in this guide.

We acknowledge a special gratitude to our friends, Steve Schmitt, Jack Padova, Anthony J. Sequeira, and Rick Boling for their time, patience and computer expertise.

Graphic images contained in this book were reproduced with the express written permission of SoftKey International, Inc.

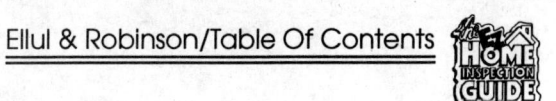

Table Of Contents

General Information

Introduction	1
Buying A Home	2
Selling Your Home	2
Current Home Owner	3
Instructions	4
Getting Bids For Repairs	6
Important Information	8
Home Cost Analysis	9

Exterior & Attic

Yard & Landscaping	11
Exterior Roof	11
Home Exterior	12
Front Entrance	13
Back Entrance	13
Side Entrance	13
Awnings Or Shutters	15
Windows, Doors & Sliding Glass Doors	15
Outdoor Patio	16
Drive & Walkway	16
Attic Area	17

Systems & Insulation

Insulation	18
Water System	20
Water Heater	21
Water Treatment	21
City Sewage System	22
Septic Tank System	22
Electrical System	23
Heating System	25
Air Conditioning System	25

Rooms & Areas

Foyer or Vestibule	27
Kitchen	28
Kitchen Appliances	30
Dining Room	32
Formal Dining Room	34
Living Room	36
Family Room	38
Library or Den	40
Lanai or Enclosed Porch	42
Master Bedroom	44
Bedroom Number Two	46
Bedroom Number Three	48
Bedroom Number Four	50
Master Bathroom	52
Bathroom Number Two	54

Rooms & Areas Cont.

Bathroom Number Three	56
Hallway	58
Stairway	59
Basement	60
Laundry Room	62

Garages & Out-Buildings

Attached Garage

Interior	65
Service Door	66
Garage Door	66

Detached Garage

Exterior Roof	68
Exterior	68
Interior	69
Service Door	70
Garage Door	70

Out-Building

Roof	72
Exterior	72
Interior	73
Drive & Walkway	74
Service Door	74
Garage Door	74

Recreational Areas

Swimming Pool	76
Whirlpool or Hot Tub	78
Pool Patio	80
Barbecue	80

Terms

Glossary	83
Real Estate Terminology	85

Records & Forms

Summary Of Estimates	89
Home Improvement Priorities	92
Repair and Improvement Summary	93
Home Information Form	97
Home Furnishings List	99
Seasonal Check List	101
Maintenance Schedule	102
Book Ordering Information	105

INTRODUCTION

This is the one and only, easy to read and understand, *E-Z Home Inspection Guide*. Our goal was to develop an organized awareness for **Buyers**, **Sellers** and **Current Home Owners**. We have created a unique guide written in everyday language, a guide both men and women can use easily to gain a greater understanding of their homes.

If you are a current homeowner, buyer or seller, you should not be too concerned about minor problems. You may unintentionally overlook a few major problems that can be very costly. Any home requires minor changes or repairs from one owner's point of view to another's. The *Guide* can help you organize, document, analyze, and maintain your valuable investment.

If you are planning to buy a home, the *Guide* can provide you with a clear and complete evaluation of your potential investment. Using the simple, one-page **Home Information Form** found in the back of the book, home buyers can easily record and analyze the important information necessary to understand the value of any home.

For current home owners, the *Guide* serves as a detailed, comprehensive journal of the home. It will enlighten you concerning hidden home expenses, help you schedule routine maintenance to safeguard against costly breakdowns, and act as a financial planner for home improvements you hope to make. The information you record in the *Guide* can be priceless if you find it necessary to negotiate a settlement with your insurance company over losses due to fire, theft or natural disaster. A combination of photographs, receipt copies and **The E-Z Home Inspection Guide** can serve as an excellent safeguard. On average, most people live in a home for seven years. It only takes a few hours to record the information that could be vital to protect your home investment.

If and when you decide to sell your home, you can impress the buyer with a complete and up-to-date maintenance record of the house and grounds. Also, this important information can possibly save you thousands of dollars in tax benefits at the time of sale.

You may love your home. You may have lived in it for several years, made payments on it, and have no intention of moving. But can you honestly recall the make or gallon capacity of your water heater, or the actual size of your bedroom? Now you can have an accurate home history, and an organized quick-reference map right at your fingertips.

Once you answer the questions in this do-it-yourself inspection guide, the book becomes a valuable, detailed analysis that will simplify the complex task of home inspection for all individuals in any region or climate.

Thank you for using *The E-Z Home Inspection Guide*. We are confident the information in our book will help you whenever you decide to buy, sell or work on your home.

Joseph A Ellul Jr.   *Bonnie D. Robinson*

Authors

Now that you have found your dream house, what are your initial impressions?

BUYING A HOME

- What kind of area is it in?
- What amenities such as shopping, schools, movies, churches and parks, are close by?
- Do you love the outside of the house and the grounds?
- Does the house have a practical floor plan?
- Can you visualize how the house will be decorated?
- Is there an area that will serve as a workshop?
- Is there an area for a garden?

First, you should read and understand *The E-Z Home Inspection Guide*. The enclosed comprehensive questions and comments will help solidify your home-construction knowledge by answering the above questions and more. The information you gain from the *Guide* will also help eliminate your concern that you may be buying another person's problems.

Ask the seller for a tour of the house, and utilize the *Home Information Form* in the *Forms* section at the back of the book to make an informed bid.

SELLING YOUR HOME

The E-Z Home Inspection Guide will inform you of the assets you may have overlooked, or the liabilities you may choose to repair before listing your property. You will be prepared to answer virtually any question a potential buyer may ask regarding the structure and maintenance of your home. Once the *Guide* is completed, the information you will provide minimizes the need for further inquiry from the buyer or the real-estate agent.

Selling Tip: Consider the buyer's first impression. Everything your potential buyer sees, hears or smells when viewing your home for the first time should be very important to you. Ask yourselves these questions before a potential buyer views your home:

- *Are the front and back yards clean and neat?* (Remove bicycles, ladders, tools, broken tree limbs, garbage or any other debris.)
- *Is the inside of the house clean and neat?* (Remove soiled laundry, dishes, newspapers, magazines and other offensive clutter. Vacuum pet hair from carpets and furniture. Your buyer may be allergic to pets.)
- *Are there any unwanted food, pet or smoke odors?* (Open all windows and air out the house. You may need to spray air freshener to give the house a clean smell.)
- *Are there any unwanted pests?* (Eliminate roaches, fleas, ants or any other unwelcome pests.)

Helpful Tip: To protect yourself and your investment, you may want to consult with an attorney when buying or selling real estate.

CURRENT HOME OWNER

As a current home owner you will have an exact and informative reference map right at your fingertips that can be useful for years to come. You can record any home improvements and/or repairs to maintain a current history of your home. The completed guide may provide valuable information if an insurance claim becomes necessary. This important information can possibly save you thousands of dollars in tax benefits when selling your home.

For More Information: Get bids from local licensed contractors, or contact your township, city or county building department for local and state building codes. You may want to contact your local police and fire departments for home security and fire safety inspections. These experienced people can guide you in the right direction to maintain your family's safety.

In many locals, utility companies offer *free energy-efficiency surveys* to homeowners, and, in some cases, will subsidize the cost of improving your home's energy efficiency. Contact your local electric or fuel-service company for information on how to take advantage of these free services.

Helpful Tip: If you cannot answer most of these questions, and/or think you may have major problems with with your home, spend the money and have a qualified home inspection company or licensed builder inspect your home for you. Ask the inspector to help you fill out any difficult parts of the guide. The cost of employing a professional will be money well spent, and can be very helpful to you in the future.

We did not attempt to evaluate the condition of your home's foundation, crawl space, footings, exterior basement wall waterproofing, or water drainage systems. These inspections are standard building procedures during construction and are approved by your local building department. If you have questions about any of the above, contact your building-department inspector, or hire a licensed contractor to inspect the problem for you.

Safety Tips: "A picture is worth a thousand words." For extra protection you should photograph or video tape your home inside and out. Photographs, along with *The E-Z Home Inspection Guide*, can be an excellent safeguard if you need to file insurance claims resulting from fire, vandalism, or weather damage. Always keep your records in a safe place away from the home, such as with a friend/family member, or in a bank safety deposit box.

Always be careful and consider safety first

Take your time and physically attempt only what you can within your personal limitations. Remain observant and pay extra attention to safety in attics, basements, or any other hazardous areas inside and outside the home. Be extremely cautious when working with electricity or using ladders.

This guide is not a test

Don't let the house overpower you. Use the *Guide* to examine your home *One Step At A Time*.

Please read each question carefully. We have added comments to help you answer many questions. These comments are not specific answers. Many questions require additional answers. Use a pencil to mark the appropriate boxes and complete the answers as honestly as possible. Use the areas marked *"Notes"* to add comments, sketches, pictures, or additional questions. Make as many extra notes as possible -- do not rely on your memory alone.

We designed the guide to help you make important and expensive decisions. If you do not know the answer to a specific question, leave it blank and investigate the answer later. The *Guide* was written to adapt to most homes in any region or climate. Please disregard any questions that do not apply to your home.

You will need the following tools for your inspection

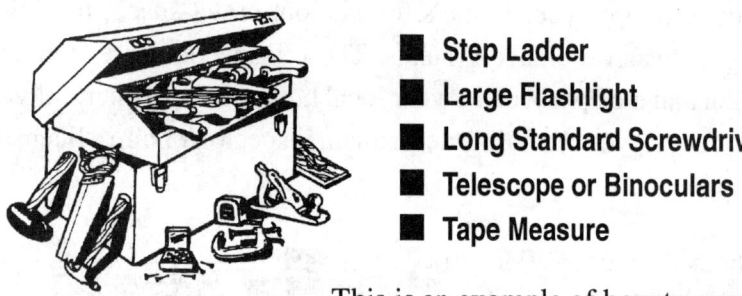

- **Step Ladder**
- **Large Flashlight**
- **Long Standard Screwdriver**
- **Telescope or Binoculars**
- **Tape Measure**

This is an example of how to approach each question:

Example:

The floor is: Wood ☐ Carpet ☐ Concrete ☐ Tile ☐ Brick ☐ Linoleum ☐ or Other_____

If the covered floor in question is *glazed brick laid over concrete*, you should check "Brick" and "Concrete," then write the word "Glazed" in the "Other_____" space. If none of the descriptions apply because the floor is bamboo, then write "Bamboo" in the "Other_____" space.

You should insert the lot survey and a photograph of the inspected home into the *Guide.* The lot survey can help you with accurate dimensions.

Helpful Tip: Before we begin your inspection, you should understand the meaning of the words ***Home Repair*** and ***Home Improvement***.

Home Repair: Suppose you were to install a new roof on your home. This would be considered a *home repair*. By replacing the old roof, you are repairing an existing part of the house. This type of repair is usually considered a basic home expense. The buyer will not total these expenses when making an offer on your home. However, the money you spent on this new roof is not in vain. A potential buyer will evaluate all the repairs you have made to your home and should take this into consideration before making an offer. Repairs do not necessarily increase the market value of a home, but can enhance the potential buyer's interest and help you to sell your home faster.

Home Improvement: Suppose you were to install an in-ground swimming pool. This would be considered a *home improvement*. The pool did not exist before. Home improvements do effect the market value of your home. You should keep an accurate record of improvements (in the *Guide*) for possible tax benefits or insurance claims.

***Notes:***

Buyers: GETTING BIDS FOR REPAIRS

Most likely the sellers will not want you to have carpenters, plumbers or electricians roaming through their home before you buy, so try to get estimates over the phone. It may take a few calls, but don't get discouraged. Most companies will work with you.

Explain to the estimator that you are looking at a home you want to buy, but first you must arrive at a total repair cost. Don't expect to get a firm price. You will only receive a ballpark figure, with both high and low costs, however, you will learn what you need to know so you can make an informed decision.

Example: Suppose you want to have the outside of the house painted. You call a painting contractor and are told estimates cannot be given over the phone, that most work is done "T & M" (time and materials). If, however, you can state the length, width and height of the area to be painted, an estimate can be made of the square footage. From this figure, the contractor can estimate how many hours and gallons of paint will be needed for one coat. Once you have the estimate, review it.

Try to review all potential repairs at this time, such as major scraping of old loose paint, caulking around windows and doors, or repairing gutters. These expenses are hard to estimate over the phone.

Let's say the estimated price was $500. If you add a 15 to 20% margin to the $500, this allows you an extra $75 or $100. Now you know it could cost between $500 and $600 to put one coat of paint on the house.

Whenever you want to paint an area, you can estimate the square footage of wall or ceiling surfaces by calculating the following figures (the paint coverage area in square feet can usually be found on the paint container):

- **Multiply the the width of the wall times the height to equal the wall's surface square footage.**
- **Multiply the room length times the width to equal the ceiling's total surface square footage.**
- **The combined total of all walls and ceiling equal the total surface square footage.**

Sellers and Current Home Owners:

Use the same method as buyers, and get as many bids as you need. Many companies still offer free home estimates. Be careful, some contractors try to get a small service charge that is refundable only when they perform their work. When getting prices, you should not be obligated to buy anything. If a company insists that you pay a service charge, shop elsewhere.

**Notes:**

---

*This space is for an area photograph, notes, drawings, or for listing the contents and features of this area, such as furniture, art, TV, stereo, location of skylights, etc. For a complete listing of home contents, use the **Home Furnishings List** in the **Forms** section at the back of the book.*

General:

Is this property in a flood area?	Yes ☐	No ☐
Is this property near a railroad track?	Yes ☐	No ☐
Is this property in a deed-restricted area?	Yes ☐	No ☐
Is this property in an airport flight pattern?	Yes ☐	No ☐
Is this property located in an historic district?	Yes ☐	No ☐
Are there any high-tension power lines nearby?	Yes ☐	No ☐
Is this property located on a dirt or gravel road?	Yes ☐	No ☐
Can the road dust drift in the direction of the house?	Yes ☐	No ☐
Is this property governed by a home owners' association?	Yes ☐	No ☐
Are there any underground storage tanks on this property?	Yes ☐	No ☐

Health Hazards:

Is there any asbestos inside or outside the house?	Yes ☐	No ☐
Are there any hazardous-waste dump sites nearby?	Yes ☐	No ☐
Is there any lead-based paint presently in this house?	Yes ☐	No ☐
Is there any urea formaldehyde insulation in this house?	Yes ☐	No ☐
Has there ever been any evidence of radon gas in this house?	Yes ☐	No ☐

Note:

The answers to all these questions should be *No*. If you answered *Yes* to any of the questions under ***Health Hazards***, seek professional advice on that subject before proceeding with the ***Guide***. Contact your county health department for more information.

HOME COST ANALYSIS

Property address:_____

City:_____State:_____Zip:_____

County:_____ Folio Number:_____

The property zoning status is:_____

Date construction was completed:_____ Date Purchased:_____

Builder's name:_____

Builder's address:_____

Builder's phone number: (____)_____ Purchase price: $_____

Monthly:

Mortgage payment: $_____

Homeowner's insurance: $_____

Water: $_____

Electric: $_____

Gas or oil: $_____

Trash removal: $_____

Yearly:

Property taxes: Year:_____ $_____   Divided by 12 = $_____

Assessments: $_____   Divided by 12 = $_____

Dues or fees: $_____   Divided by 12 = $_____

Other expenses: $_____   Divided by 12 = $_____

Your Total Monthly Expenses Are: $_____

Notes:

---

*This space is for an area photograph, notes, drawings, or for listing the contents and features of this area, such as furniture, art, TV, stereo, location of skylights, etc. For a complete listing of home contents, use the **Home Furnishings List** in the **Forms** section at the back of the book.*

YARD AND LANDSCAPE

Lot size: Length_____ X Width_____ = Square Footage_____

Your lot survey can help you with precise lot dimensions.

Fencing is: Wood ☐   Metal ☐   Cyclone ☐   Concrete ☐   Stone ☐   None ☐
Other_____

Professionally landscaped? *(Does the yard need work or replacement?)*   Yes ☐   No ☐

Are sprinklers installed? Yes ☐ No ☐   Working properly? Yes ☐ No ☐   Automatic ☐   Manual ☐

Will rain water drain away from the house?   Yes ☐   No ☐
(Ground should angle downward from the house.)

Over-all condition: Well maintained ☐   Needs repair ☐

EXTERIOR ROOF

Danger: <u>Never climb on the roof! Leave this to the professionals.</u> To inspect the roof from the ground, stand back and look carefully. If you cannot see the roof's details very well, use a telescope or binoculars.

Construction is:
Wood ☐   Asphalt ☐   Shingle ☐   Asbestos ☐
Cement ☐   Slate ☐   Tile ☐   Metal ☐
Other_____
_____

Estimated age of roof: Months:_____ Years:_____
Has the roof been recently repaired?   Yes ☐   No ☐
Is there roof ventilation? *(Keeps attic cool and prolongs roof life.)*   Yes ☐   No ☐
Is there a screen on top of the chimney? *(Keeps animals outside.)*   Yes ☐   No ☐
Are there any tree limbs on the roof? *(Avoid roof damage.)*   Yes ☐   No ☐
Does the roof sag or bow? *(Roof may be weak. Contact a roofer.)*   Yes ☐   No ☐
Are there any roof leaks? *(Check inside ceilings for water leaks.)*   Yes ☐   No ☐
Flashing condition is: *(Prevents water leaks)*   Maintained ☐   Needs repair ☐
Seals around vents are: *(Prevents water leaks)*   Maintained ☐   Needs repair ☐
Over-all condition: Well maintained ☐   Needs repair ☐
Check here if the roof is snow covered and cannot be examined. ☐

HOME EXTERIOR

Dimensions: Length_____ Width_____ Height_____

Your lot survey can help you with precise home exterior dimensions.

Construction is: Brick ☐ Aluminum ☐ Vinyl ☐ Wood ☐ Shingle ☐ Asbestos ☐ Block ☐
Stucco ☐ Stone ☐ Other_____

Paint and caulking is: Maintained ☐   Repair ☐
(Will seal & prevent deterioration. Also keeps bugs and moisture out. Check caulking around faucet bibs, outlets, lights, and dryer vent.)

Gutters & downspouts are: Maintained ☐   Repair ☐
(Are they cleaned out, secure and functional?)

Total faucet bibs: _____

Total electrical outlets (GFCIs): _____

Over-all condition: Well maintained ☐   Needs repair ☐

Notes: _____

---

*This space is for an area photograph, notes, drawings, or for listing the contents and features of this area, such as furniture, art, TV, stereo, location of skylights, etc. For a complete listing of home contents, use the **Home Furnishings List** in the **Forms** section at the back of the book.*

FRONT ENTRANCE

Approach construction is: Concrete ☐ Brick ☐ Wood ☐ Metal ☐

Other_____

Do the door and lock(s) work properly?	Yes ☐	No ☐
Are the porch steps okay? *(Comfortable and safe to walk up and down.)*	Yes ☐	No ☐
Is there a safety handrail? *(Better safe than sorry.)*	Yes ☐	No ☐
Is there artificial lighting? *(Can you see the stairs at night?)*	Yes ☐	No ☐
Is there a screen or storm door? Yes ☐ No ☐ Is the door working properly?	Yes ☐	No ☐
Is the doorbell working? *(Is sound audible throughout the house?)*	Yes ☐	No ☐

BACK ENTRANCE

Approach construction is: Concrete ☐ Brick ☐ Wood ☐ Metal ☐

Other_____

Do the door and lock(s) work properly?		Yes ☐	No ☐
Are the porch steps okay? *(Comfortable and safe to walk up and down.)*		Yes ☐	No ☐
Is there a safety handrail? *(Better safe than sorry.)*		Yes ☐	No ☐
Is there artificial lighting? *(Can you see the stairs at night?)*		Yes ☐	No ☐
Is there a screen or storm door? Yes ☐ No ☐ Is the door working properly?		Yes ☐	No ☐
Is the doorbell working? *(Is sound audible throughout the house?)*	None ☐	Yes ☐	No ☐

SIDE ENTRANCE

Approach construction is: Concrete ☐ Brick ☐ Wood ☐ Metal ☐

Other_____

Do the door and lock(s) work properly?		Yes ☐	No ☐
Are the porch steps okay? *(Comfortable and safe to walk up and down.)*		Yes ☐	No ☐
Is there a safety handrail? *(Better safe than sorry.)*		Yes ☐	No ☐
Is there artificial lighting? *(Can you see the stairs at night?)*		Yes ☐	No ☐
Is there a screen or storm door? Yes ☐ No ☐ Is the door working properly?		Yes ☐	No ☐
Is the door bell working? *(Is sound audible throughout the house?)*	None ☐	Yes ☐	No ☐

Notes:

---

*This space is for an area photograph, notes, drawings, or for listing the contents and features of this area, such as furniture, art, TV, stereo, location of skylights, etc. For a complete listing of home contents, use the **Home Furnishings List** in the **Forms** section at the back of the book.*

AWNINGS OR SHUTTERS

Construction is: Metal ☐ Canvas ☐ Wood ☐ None ☐
Other_____

Constructed for: Decoration ☐ Shade ☐ To prevent vandalism ☐
To prevent weather damage ☐ Other:_____
_____

Do the awnings or shutters work properly? Yes ☐ No ☐

Over-all condition: Well maintained ☐ Needs repair ☐

WINDOWS - DOORS SLIDING GLASS DOORS

Construction of windows is: Metal ☐ Wood ☐ Aluminum ☐ Vinyl ☐
Other_____

Construction of doors is: Metal ☐ Wood ☐ Aluminum ☐ Vinyl ☐
Other_____

Construction of sliding doors is: Metal ☐ Wood ☐ Aluminum ☐ Vinyl ☐
Other_____

Window manufacturer's name is:_____

Door manufacturer's name is: _____

Sliding door manufacturer's name is:_____

Over-all condition: Well maintained ☐ Needs repair ☐

If the screens or storm windows are not in place, where are they located?_____
_____

Helpful Tip: When you want to wash your storm windows or screens, location reference marks can help you find the correct windows without the guesswork. Scratch or paint (fingernail polish usually works well) a small number or letter on the window frames and a corresponding number or letter on the storm windows or screens *before* you remove them. When rehanging them, look for the corresponding marks.

OUTDOOR PATIO

Construction is: Brick ☐ Stone ☐ Concrete ☐ Asphalt ☐ Wood ☐
Other _____

Is there artificial lighting? *(Can you see for safety?)* Yes ☐ No ☐

Are there electrical outlets? *(Are they protected by GFCIs?)* Yes ☐ No ☐

Is the area screen enclosed? *(Do the screens, doors and windows work?)* Yes ☐ No ☐

Over-all condition: Well maintained ☐ Needs repair ☐

DRIVE & WALKWAY

Construction is: Brick ☐ Stone ☐ Concrete ☐ Asphalt ☐ Wood ☐
Other _____

Is there artificial lighting? *(Can you see the driveway at night?)* Yes ☐ No ☐

Over-all condition: Well maintained ☐ Needs repair ☐

Helpful Tip: The ground should angle downward from the house. Will the drive and walkway rain water drain away from the house?

Check here if the drive and walkway are snow covered and cannot be examined. ☐

Notes: _____

ATTIC AREA

DANGER:* Always be careful.** There is no need to crawl around in the attic to do this inspection. Most inspections can be done at the door opening. Use a large flashlight or trouble light and inspect any potential lumber dry rot first. If you must enter, please be sure the wood is firm before going into the attic, and ***only walk on or grasp secure wood or metal. Be aware that you are walking on the topside support structure of a fragile ceiling below.

Attic entrance is in: Hallway ☐ Closet ☐ Garage ☐ Bedroom ☐ Bathroom ☐
Other_____

You enter the attic through: Stairway & door ☐ Ceiling access panel ☐ No access ☐

Is the attic floor covered with plywood? Yes ☐ No ☐

Is insulation visible throughout the attic? Yes ☐ No ☐

Is there insulation throughout the attic floor? Yes ☐ No ☐

Is there any lumber dry rot? *(The wood is soft or falls apart easily.)* Yes ☐ No ☐

Are there any termites? *(If you don't know, contact a professional.)* Yes ☐ No ☐

Is there any evidence of animals? *(Squirrels, mice, raccoons.)* Yes ☐ No ☐

Is there artificial lighting? *(More light than a flashlight.)* Yes ☐ No ☐

Dampness? *(If "yes," it promotes dry rot, so check for roof leaks.)* Yes ☐ No ☐

Is there natural air ventilation? Yes ☐ No ☐
(Air flow is important to keep dampness out of the area, keep lumber in a dry condition, and help prolong the life of roofing materials.)

Natural air vents are in the: Eaves ☐ Middle of roof ☐ Top of roof ☐ Outside wall ☐
Other_____

Is there a ventilation fan? *(Motor driven or temperature controlled?)* Yes ☐ No ☐
(A temperature-controlled ventilation fan system is a great way to control the air flow in the attic.)

Insulation thickness: (in inches)_____

Over-all condition: Well maintained ☐ Needs repair ☐

INSULATION

Is there any insulation installed?   Yes ☐   No ☐

Type is: Wool ☐   Fiberglass ☐   Cellulose ☐   Blanket ☐   Other _____

Approximate thickness and "R" values are: Attic: _____

Walls: _____

Floors: _____

The manufacturer's name is: _____

Helpful Tips: More insulation is better than not enough. Check with your lumber or hardware store for the recommended "R" value in your area. You may want to take a very small amount of the existing insulation and the estimated thickness (in inches) with you. This will help you find out the type of product and "R" value.

An easy way to check for insulation in the exterior walls from inside is to remove a cover plate from a TV or phone jack and look between the box and the wall's edge to see if insulation exists. To estimate its thickness, measure the distance between the window glass and the wall's edge. Some interior walls may have no insulation.

In many locals, utility companies offer *free energy-efficiency surveys* to homeowners. In some cases they will subsidize the cost of improving your home's energy efficiency. Contact your local electric or fuel-service company for information on how to take advantage of these free services.

Estimated "R" Value for:

Attics:	North 30 to 38	South 26 to 30
Walls:	North 19	South 13 to 19
Floors:	North 19 to 22	South 11 to 22

Notes: _____

 **Notes:**

*This space is for an area photograph, notes, drawings, or for listing the contents and features of this area, such as furniture, art, TV, stereo, location of skylights, etc. For a complete listing of home contents, use the **Home Furnishings List** in the **Forms** section at the back of the book.*

WATER SYSTEM

Is city water connected to the building? Yes ☐ No ☐

What area do you purchase your water from?_____

Where is the water meter located?_____

Is well water connected to the building? Yes ☐ No ☐

The well's installation date was: Month____Day____Year____

The location of the well is:_____

Do you have a completed report from a laboratory or health department on the well water's sanitary status? Yes ☐ No ☐

Is the well working properly? Yes ☐ No ☐

The pump was last serviced on: (A)_____ (B)_____ (C)_____ (D)_____ (E)_____

Service company:_____ Phone: (___)_____

Do you ever run out of water? Yes ☐ No ☐

The well depth is:_____feet Width is:_____inches

Is the water pressure okay? *(Approximately four gallons per minute.)* Yes ☐ No ☐

Helpful Tip: You may want to evaluate your water pressure (gallons per minute) at the bath tub or outside water spigot. If you live in an area that has a limited city water supply and restricts water usage, your gallons per minute may be lower.

Well water pressure may vary. Allow the water to run a few minutes to see if the water pressure is constant. If the water pressure is low at one sink, remove the existing screen from the end of the faucet and clean it. You can also turn on the faucet without the screen to see if the pressure increases.

WATER TREATMENT

Is there a water purification system? Yes ☐ No ☐

Is the system working properly? Yes ☐ No ☐

The system installation date was: Month:_____ Day:_____ Year:_____

Service company:_____ Phone: (___)_____

Types of equipment installed are: Water softener ☐ Sand filter ☐ Carbon filter ☐
Chlorination ☐ Other_____

WATER HEATER

Are there any water leaks? *(If yes, where?)*   Yes ☐   No ☐

The water heater's total gallon capacity is:_____
(Allow 10 gallons per person using gas or oil, You may need a little more for electric.)

Where is the water heater located?_____

Where is the main shut-off valve located?_____

The manufacturer's name is:_____

Model #_____ **Serial #**_____

The heater's installation date was: Month_____ Day_____ Year_____

Last date serviced was: (A)_____ (B)_____ (C)_____ (D)_____ (E)_____

Service company:_____ **Phone:** (____)_____

Is there an owner's manual? *(Can be useful for part replacement.)*   Yes ☐   No ☐

Is the system working okay? *(If "no," get a price for repair.)*   Yes ☐   No ☐

Is there an insulating cover? *(Can help reduce fuel costs.)*   Yes ☐   No ☐

Is the pressure relief valve okay? *(The valve releases excess tank pressure.)*   Yes ☐   No ☐

System operates on: Electricity ☐   Natural gas ☐   Liquid propane (LP gas) ☐   Oil ☐

                Solar collector ☐   Other_____

Over-all condition: Well maintained ☐   Needs repair ☐

Helpful Tip: Is there an automatic (on/off) timer installed on your electric water heater? Ask yourself if you use hot water when you are asleep or at work. This inexpensive wonder can save you a considerable amount of money on electric bills.

Where is the location of the gas meter, LP gas tank, or oil tank?_____

_____

_____

_____

(If needed, take a picture or draw a diagram on a note page to show the exact location.)

CITY SEWAGE SYSTEM

Is the building connected to the city sewage system?   Yes ☐   No ☐

Is the system working properly? *(If "no," get a price for repair)*   Yes ☐   No ☐

SEPTIC TANK SYSTEM

Is the building connected to a septic system?   Yes ☐   No ☐

The septic tank installation date was: Month:_____ Day:_____ Year:_____

The tank was last cleaned on: (A)_____ (B)_____ (C)_____ (D)_____ (E)_____

Service company:_____ Phone: (____)_____

The septic tank size is: 500 gallon ☐   750 gallon ☐   1,000 gallon ☐   Other_____

Type is: Concrete ☐   Metal ☐   Other_____

Location of the septic tank and drain field is:_____
_____
_____
_____

Are the septic tank & drain field working properly?   Yes ☐   No ☐
(If "no," get a price for repair.)

Has a liquid ever flowed out of the lawn?   Yes ☐   No ☐
(If "yes," the drain field may be broken. Get a price for repair.)

Over-all condition: Well maintained ☐   Needs repair ☐

*Notes:*_____

ELECTRICAL SYSTEM

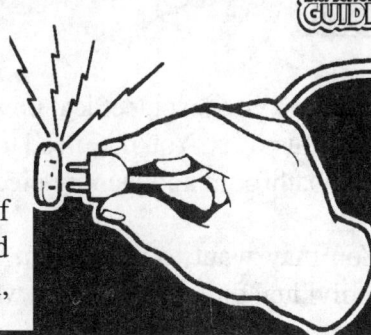

DANGER: **Do you really understand electricity?** If you are not sure, don't take the risk. You may want to have a licensed electrician inspect your home to prevent any accidental electrocution, bodily injury or fires.

Are there any old or frayed wires? *(Do not touch. Call an electrician.)*   Yes ☐   No ☐

Where is the electric meter located? _____

Where is the fuse box located?   Garage ☐   Kitchen ☐   Basement ☐   Hallway ☐
   Outside ☐   Other _____

What is the number of circuits in use? *(Total fuses or breakers in the fuse box.):* _____

The total house amperage is: 60 ☐   100 ☐   150 ☐   200 ☐   300 ☐   400 ☐
(The service main fuse is this amount.)

The total voltage is: 220/240 ☐   110/120 ☐
*(**Two** large wires from the electric pole to the house is 110/120;*
***Three** Large wires is 220/240, which is today's standard.)*

Helpful Tip: Observe the wires coming from the electric pole to your house. The first large wire is 110 volts; the second large wire is 110 volts; the third large wire is the ground. This equals 220/240 volts. If you do not see any electric or telephone poles, your 220/240 volt service main power lines are underground and out of sight.

Are the fuses or breakers in the main box labeled for each area location?   Yes ☐   No ☐
(They should be marked, in or outside the panel box.)

Are the outlets grounded? *(If grounded, each outlet has three holes.)*   Yes ☐   No ☐
(If the outlets are grounded, the house is most likely a 220/240 system.)

Do the fuses blow often?   Yes ☐   No ☐
(If "yes," something is wrong on the circuit. Call an electrician.)

Are Ground Fault Circuit Interrupters (GFCIs) installed?   Yes ☐   No ☐
(A safety device for wet locations - bathrooms, kitchens, etc.)

Over-all Condition: Well-maintained ☐   Needs repair ☐

Helpful Tip: The home's grounding system should be correct if Ground Fault Circuit Interrupters are installed and work properly. GFCI outlets have circuit breakers built in to them. Multiple outlets may connect to one GFCI breaker or GFCI outlet. The easy way to locate other GFCI-protected electrical outlets is to:

- ■ Test all area outlets to make sure they are working properly.
- ■ Press the GFCI's "TEST" button to isolate the protected outlets.
- ■ Check for the absence of electricity at other outlets. All of the disabled outlets are connected to the GFCI.
- ■ Press the "RESET: button to regain electrical power.

Suppose you lost electrical power at an outlet and cannot find a blown fuse or circuit breaker in the main fuse box. You may need to "RESET" the corresponding GFCI outlet to regain power. Example: The bathroom and laundry electrical plugs may be connected to one GFCI breaker or GFCI outlet.

You may want to purchase a small, self-contained (three-prong) plug-in testing device to check individual outlets for correct wiring and grounding. They are safe, easy to use and available at most electrical or hardware stores.

Notes: _____

---

*This space is for an area photograph, notes, drawings, or for listing the contents and features of this area, such as furniture, art, TV, stereo, location of skylights, etc. For a complete listing of home contents, use the **Home Furnishings List** in the **Forms** section at the back of the book.*

HEATING AND AIR CONDITIONING

Are the heat and air-conditioning system one central unit? Yes ☐ No ☐
Do you have the owner's manual? *(Useful for part replacement)* Yes ☐ No ☐
The central unit location is:_____
Fuel company:_____
Phone: (____)_____

HEATING SYSTEM

The name of the system is:_____
Serial #_____ Model #_____
The system's installation date was: Month:_____ Day:_____ Year:_____
Last date serviced was: (A)_____ (B)_____ (C)_____ (D)_____ (E)_____
Service company:_____ Phone (____)_____
System operates on: Gas ☐ Oil ☐ Electric ☐ Forced air ☐ Gravity ☐ Steam ☐ Water ☐
Radiant ☐ Other_____

The blower motor size is: _____ Horse Power

Are filters installed?   Yes ☐ No ☐
(Filters keep dust out of the blower and motor and help prevent repairs.)

Is the system working properly? *(If "no," get price for repair.)*   Yes ☐ No ☐
Is the thermostat(s) working? *(Controls house temperature.)*   Yes ☐ No ☐
Is there a humidifier? *(Adds moisture into the air. Working properly?)*   Yes ☐ No ☐

Over-all Condition: Well-maintained ☐ Needs repair ☐

AIR CONDITIONING SYSTEM

The name of the system is:_____
Serial #_____ Model #_____
The system's installation date was: Month:_____ Day:_____ Year:_____
Last date serviced was: (A)_____ (B)_____ (C)_____ (D)_____ (E)_____
Service company:_____ Phone (____)_____
System operates on: Gas ☐ Oil ☐ Electric ☐ Forced air ☐ Gravity ☐ Steam ☐ Water ☐
Radiant ☐ Other_____

The blower motor size is: _____ Horse Power

Are filters installed?   Yes ☐   No ☐
(Filters keep dust out of the blower and motor and help prevent repairs.)

Is the system working properly? *(if "no," get price for repair.)*   Yes ☐   No ☐

Is the thermostat(s) working? *(controls house temperature.)*   Yes ☐   No ☐

Over-all Condition: Well-maintained ☐   Needs repair ☐

Helpful Tip: Is there an automatic (on/off) timer installed on your heating and air-conditioning system's thermostat? Ask yourself if you need to maintain the same temperature in the house when you are asleep or at work. This inexpensive wonder can save you money on your electric and fuel bills.

Test the heating or air-conditioning system's performance. You may want to have a professional licensed company inspect it for you. Heat exchanges, motors and compressors can be expensive to repair or replace.

Notes: _____

---

*This space is for an area photograph, notes, drawings, or for listing the contents and features of this area, such as furniture, art, TV, stereo, location of skylights, etc. For a complete listing of home contents, use the **Home Furnishings List** in the **Forms** section at the back of the book.*

FOYER OR VESTIBULE

Dimensions: Length_____ Width_____ Height_____

The floor is: Wood ☐   Carpet ☐   Concrete ☐   Tile ☐   Brick ☐   Linoleum ☐
Other _____

The walls are: Plaster ☐   Drywall ☐   Wood ☐   Tile ☐   Wallpaper ☐
Other _____

The ceiling is: Plaster ☐   Drywall ☐   Wood ☐   Tile ☐   Wallpaper ☐
Other _____

Approximate

Floor color is:_____
Wall color is:_____
Ceiling color is:_____

Do you need to replace the floor? Are there any cracks, holes or squeaks?

Floor condition is:	Maintained ☐	Repair ☐
Wall condition is:	Maintained ☐	Repair ☐
Ceiling condition is:	Maintained ☐	Repair ☐
Artificial lighting is:	Maintained ☐	Repair ☐
Door condition is:	Maintained ☐	Repair ☐

Is there a ceiling fan(s) *(Operating properly?)*   Yes ☐   No ☐
Is there fan lighting? *(Does it work? Pull chain or switch?)*   Yes ☐   No ☐
Any daylight sunshine? *(Can you see without artificial lighting?)*   Yes ☐   No ☐
Do the windows work properly? *(Is there any broken or cracked glass?)*   Yes ☐   No ☐

Total windows in this area: One ☐   Two ☐   Three ☐   Four ☐   More_____   None ☐

Total windows, screens or storms: Damaged_____   Missing_____

Window treatments: Drapes ☐   Shutters ☐   Blinds ☐   Verticals ☐   None ☐

Total electric outlets are:_____   **Total heat or air registers in this area are:**_____

Over-all Condition: Well-maintained ☐   Needs repair ☐

Notes:

KITCHEN

Dimensions:	Length_____	Width_____		Height_____	
The floor is:	Wood ☐ Carpet ☐	Concrete ☐	Tile ☐	Brick ☐	Linoleum ☐
	Other _____				
The walls are:	Plaster ☐ Drywall ☐	Wood ☐	Tile ☐	Wallpaper ☐	
	Other _____				
The ceiling is:	Plaster ☐ Drywall ☐	Wood ☐	Tile ☐	Wallpaper ☐	
	Other _____				
The cabinets are:	Wood ☐	Metal ☐		Plastic Laminate ☐	
	Other _____				
Counter top is:	Wood ☐ Metal ☐	Plastic Laminate ☐		Tile ☐	
	Other _____				

Approximate

Floor color is:_____

Wall color is:_____

Ceiling color is:_____

Do you need to replace the floor? Are there any cracks, holes or squeaks?

Floor condition is:	Maintained ☐	Repair ☐
Wall condition is:	Maintained ☐	Repair ☐
Ceiling condition is:	Maintained ☐	Repair ☐
Door condition is:	Maintained ☐	Repair ☐
Cabinet condition is:	Maintained ☐	Repair ☐
Counter top condition is:	Maintained ☐	Repair ☐
Sink condition is:	Maintained ☐	Repair ☐
Artificial lighting is:	Maintained ☐	Repair ☐

Do the cabinet door hinges work? *(All the same style? Any loose?)*	Yes ☐	No ☐
Do the cabinet drawers work? *(Sliding guides work properly?)*	Yes ☐	No ☐
Intercom system? *(Working properly throughout the house?)*	Yes ☐	No ☐
Are outlets on GFCIs? *(Better to be safe than sorry.)*	Yes ☐	No ☐
Is there a pantry? *(Do you have enough room for storage?)*	Yes ☐	No ☐
Is there hot and cold water? *(Check under the sink for leaks.)*	Yes ☐	No ☐
Is the water pressure okay? *(Approximately four gallons per minute.)*	Yes ☐	No ☐
Is there a ceiling fan(s)? *(Operating properly?)*	Yes ☐	No ☐

Is there fan lighting? *(Does it work? Pull chain or switch?)*	Yes ☐ No ☐
Any daylight sunshine? *(Can you see without artificial lighting?)*	Yes ☐ No ☐
Do the windows work properly? *(Is there any broken or cracked glass?)*	Yes ☐ No ☐

Total windows in this area: One ☐ Two ☐ Three ☐ Four ☐ More _____ None ☐

Total windows, screens or storms: Damaged _____ Missing _____

Window treatments: Drapes ☐ Shutters ☐ Blinds ☐ Verticals ☐ None ☐
Other _____

Total electric outlets are: _____ **Total heat or air registers in this area are:** _____

Over-all Condition: Well-maintained ☐ Needs repair ☐

Is there a TV or cable connector? *(Do you need one in this room?)* Yes ☐ No ☐

Is there a telephone connector? *(Do you need one in this room?)* Yes ☐ No ☐

Is there a wood-burning stove in this room? Yes ☐ No ☐

Is there a fireplace in this room? Yes ☐ No ☐

Fireplace construction is: Stone ☐ Brick ☐ Tile ☐ Metal ☐
Other _____

Fireplace enclosure is: Glass doors ☐ Screen ☐ None ☐
Other _____

Damper is: Maintained ☐ Repair ☐
(The damper is a metal plate inside the chimney necessary to close chimney flue.)

Fireplace or wood-burning stove are: Maintained ☐ Repair ☐

Notes: _____

KITCHEN APPLIANCES

Will kitchen appliances remain when you sell your home?   Yes ☐   No ☐

Do you have the owner's manuals? *(Useful for part replacement)*   Yes ☐   No ☐

List the manufacturer's name	Date purchased	Working okay?
_____ (Stove & oven combo)	_____	Yes ☐ No ☐
_____ (Wall oven)	_____	Yes ☐ No ☐
_____ (Refrigerator)	_____	Yes ☐ No ☐
_____ (Dishwasher)	_____	Yes ☐ No ☐
_____ (Trash compactor)	_____	Yes ☐ No ☐
_____ (Microwave)	_____	Yes ☐ No ☐
_____ (Blender)	_____	Yes ☐ No ☐
_____ (Toaster)	_____	Yes ☐ No ☐
_____ (Garbage disposal)	_____	Yes ☐ No ☐
_____ (Telephone)	_____	Yes ☐ No ☐
_____	_____	Yes ☐ No ☐

Is there a fire extinguisher? *(ABC type dry-chemical for all fires.)*   Yes ☐   No ☐

Is there an exhaust fan? *(Used to remove smoke and odors.)*   Yes ☐   No ☐

Exhaust fan's condition: *(Are filter & grease trap clean?)*   Maintained ☐   Repair ☐

Stove and/or oven is: Natural gas ☐   Liquid propane (LP) gas ☐   Electric ☐
Other_____

Over-all Condition: Well-maintained ☐   Needs repair ☐

Notes:

---

*This space is for an area photograph, notes, drawings, or for listing the contents and features of this area, such as furniture, art, TV, stereo, location of skylights, etc. For a complete listing of home contents, use the **Home Furnishings List** in the **Forms** section at the back of the book.*

DINING ROOM

Dimensions: Length_____ Width_____ Height_____

The floor is: Wood ☐ Carpet ☐ Concrete ☐ Tile ☐ Brick ☐ Linoleum ☐
Other _____

The walls are: Plaster ☐ Drywall ☐ Wood ☐ Tile ☐ Wallpaper ☐
Other _____

The ceiling is: Plaster ☐ Drywall ☐ Wood ☐ Tile ☐ Wallpaper ☐
Other _____

Approximate
Floor color is:_____
Wall color is:_____
Ceiling color is:_____

Do you need to replace the floor? Are there any cracks, holes or squeaks?

Floor condition is: Maintained ☐ Repair ☐
Wall condition is: Maintained ☐ Repair ☐
Ceiling condition is: Maintained ☐ Repair ☐
Artificial lighting is: Maintained ☐ Repair ☐
Door condition is: Maintained ☐ Repair ☐

Is there a ceiling fan(s)? *(Operating properly?)* Yes ☐ No ☐

Is there fan lighting? *(Does it work? Pull chain or switch?)* Yes ☐ No ☐

Any daylight sunshine? *(Can you see without artificial lighting?)* Yes ☐ No ☐

Do the windows work properly? *(Is there any broken or cracked glass?)* Yes ☐ No ☐

Total windows in this area: One ☐ Two ☐ Three ☐ Four ☐ More____ None ☐

Total windows, screens or storms: Damaged_____ Missing_____

Window treatments: Drapes ☐ Shutters ☐ Blinds ☐ Verticals ☐ None ☐

Total electric outlets are:_____ **Total heat or air registers in this area are:**_____

Over-all Condition: Well-maintained ☐ Needs repair ☐

Is there a TV or cable connector? *(Do you need one in this room?)*   Yes ☐   No ☐

Is there a telephone connector? *(Do you need one in this room?)*   Yes ☐   No ☐

Is there a wood-burning stove in this room?   Yes ☐   No ☐

Is there a fireplace in this room?   Yes ☐   No ☐

Fireplace construction is: Stone ☐   Brick ☐   Tile ☐   Metal ☐   Other_____

Fireplace enclosure is: Glass doors ☐   Screen ☐   None ☐   Other_____

Damper is: Maintained ☐   Repair ☐
(The damper is a metal plate inside the chimney necessary to close chimney flue.)

Fireplace or wood-burning stove are: Maintained ☐   Repair ☐

Notes: _____

---

*This space is for an area photograph, notes, drawings, or for listing the contents and features of this area, such as furniture, art, TV, stereo, location of skylights, etc. For a complete listing of home contents, use the **Home Furnishings List** in the **Forms** section at the back of the book.*

FORMAL DINING ROOM

Dimensions: Length_____ Width_____ Height_____

The floor is: Wood ☐ Carpet ☐ Concrete ☐ Tile ☐ Brick ☐ Linoleum ☐
Other _____

The walls are: Plaster ☐ Drywall ☐ Wood ☐ Tile ☐ Wallpaper ☐
Other _____

The ceiling is: Plaster ☐ Drywall ☐ Wood ☐ Tile ☐ Wallpaper ☐
Other _____

Approximate
Floor color is:_____
Wall color is:_____
Ceiling color is:_____

Do you need to replace the floor? Are there any cracks, holes or squeaks?

Floor condition is: Maintained ☐ Repair ☐

Wall condition is: Maintained ☐ Repair ☐

Ceiling condition is: Maintained ☐ Repair ☐

Artificial lighting is: Maintained ☐ Repair ☐

Door condition is: Maintained ☐ Repair ☐

Is there a ceiling fan(s) *(Operating properly?)* Yes ☐ No ☐

Is there fan lighting? *(Does it work? Pull chain or switch?)* Yes ☐ No ☐

Any daylight sunshine? *(Can you see without artificial lighting?)* Yes ☐ No ☐

Do the windows work properly? *(Is there any broken or cracked glass?)* Yes ☐ No ☐

Total windows in this area: One ☐ Two ☐ Three ☐ Four ☐ More_____ None ☐

Total windows, screens or storms: Damaged_____ Missing_____

Window treatments: Drapes ☐ Shutters ☐ Blinds ☐ Verticals ☐ None ☐

Total electric outlets are:_____ **Total heat or air registers in this area are:**_____

Over-all Condition: Well-maintained ☐ Needs repair ☐

Is there a TV or cable connector? *(Do you need one in this room?)*   Yes ☐   No ☐

Is there a telephone connector? *(Do you need one in this room?)*   Yes ☐   No ☐

Is there a wood-burning stove in this room?   Yes ☐   No ☐

Is there a fireplace in this room?   Yes ☐   No ☐

Fireplace construction is: Stone ☐   Brick ☐   Tile ☐   Metal ☐   Other _____

Fireplace enclosure is: Glass doors ☐   Screen ☐   None ☐   Other _____

Damper is: Maintained ☐   Repair ☐
(The damper is a metal plate inside the chimney necessary to close chimney flue.)

Fireplace or wood-burning stove are: Maintained ☐   Repair ☐

Notes: _____

---

*This space is for an area photograph, notes, drawings, or for listing the contents and features of this area, such as furniture, art, TV, stereo, location of skylights, etc. For a complete listing of home contents, use the **Home Furnishings List** in the **Forms** section at the back of the book.*

LIVING ROOM

Dimensions: Length_____ Width_____ Height_____

The floor is: Wood ☐ Carpet ☐ Concrete ☐ Tile ☐ Brick ☐ Linoleum ☐
Other _____

The walls are Plaster ☐ Drywall ☐ Wood ☐ Tile ☐ Wallpaper ☐
Other _____

The ceiling is: Plaster ☐ Drywall ☐ Wood ☐ Tile ☐ Wallpaper ☐
Other _____

Approximate Floor color is:_____

Wall color is:_____

Ceiling color is:_____

Do you need to replace the floor? Are there any cracks, holes or squeaks?

Floor condition is: Maintained ☐ Repair ☐

Wall condition is: Maintained ☐ Repair ☐

Ceiling condition is: Maintained ☐ Repair ☐

Artificial lighting is: Maintained ☐ Repair ☐

Door condition is: Maintained ☐ Repair ☐

Is there a ceiling fan(s) *(Operating properly?)* Yes ☐ No ☐

Is there fan lighting? *(Does it work? Pull chain or switch?)* Yes ☐ No ☐

Any daylight sunshine? *(Can you see without artificial lighting?)* Yes ☐ No ☐

Do the windows work properly? *(Is there any broken or cracked glass?)* Yes ☐ No ☐

Total windows in this area: One ☐ Two ☐ Three ☐ Four ☐ More_____ None ☐

Total windows, screens or storms: Damaged_____ Missing_____

Window treatments: Drapes ☐ Shutters ☐ Blinds ☐ Verticals ☐ None ☐

Total electric outlets are:_____ **Total heat or air registers in this area are:**_____

Over-all Condition: Well-maintained ☐ Needs repair ☐

Is there a TV or cable connector? *(Do you need one in this room?)*   Yes ☐   No ☐

Is there a telephone connector? *(Do you need one in this room?)*   Yes ☐   No ☐

Is there a wood-burning stove in this room?   Yes ☐   No ☐

Is there a fireplace in this room?   Yes ☐   No ☐

Fireplace construction is: Stone ☐   Brick ☐   Tile ☐   Metal ☐   Other_____

Fireplace enclosure is: Glass doors ☐   Screen ☐   None ☐   Other_____

Damper is: Maintained ☐   Repair ☐
(The damper is a metal plate inside the chimney necessary to close chimney flue.)

Fireplace or wood-burning stove are: Maintained ☐   Repair ☐

Notes: _____

---

*This space is for an area photograph, notes, drawings, or for listing the contents and features of this area, such as furniture, art, TV, stereo, location of skylights, etc. For a complete listing of home contents, use the **Home Furnishings List** in the **Forms** section at the back of the book.*

FAMILY ROOM

Dimensions: Length_____ Width_____ Height_____

The floor is: Wood ☐ Carpet ☐ Concrete ☐ Tile ☐ Brick ☐ Linoleum ☐
Other _____

The walls are: Plaster ☐ Drywall ☐ Wood ☐ Tile ☐ Wallpaper ☐
Other _____

The ceiling is: Plaster ☐ Drywall ☐ Wood ☐ Tile ☐ Wallpaper ☐
Other _____

Approximate Floor color is:_____

Wall color is:_____

Ceiling color is:_____

Do you need to replace the floor? Are there any cracks, holes or squeaks?

Floor condition is: Maintained ☐ Repair ☐

Wall condition is: Maintained ☐ Repair ☐

Ceiling condition is: Maintained ☐ Repair ☐

Artificial lighting is: Maintained ☐ Repair ☐

Door condition is: Maintained ☐ Repair ☐

Is there a ceiling fan(s) *(Operating properly?)* Yes ☐ No ☐

Is there fan lighting? *(Does it work? Pull chain or switch?)* Yes ☐ No ☐

Any daylight sunshine? *(Can you see without artificial lighting?)* Yes ☐ No ☐

Do the windows work properly? *(Is there any broken or cracked glass?)* Yes ☐ No ☐

Total windows in this area: One ☐ Two ☐ Three ☐ Four ☐ More_____ None ☐

Total windows, screens or storms: Damaged_____ Missing_____

Window treatments: Drapes ☐ Shutters ☐ Blinds ☐ Verticals ☐ None ☐

Total electric outlets are:_____ **Total heat or air registers in this area are:_____**

Over-all Condition: Well-maintained ☐ Needs repair ☐

Is there a TV or cable connector? *(Do you need one in this room?)*   Yes ☐   No ☐

Is there a telephone connector? *(Do you need one in this room?)*   Yes ☐   No ☐

Is there a wood-burning stove in this room?   Yes ☐   No ☐

Is there a fireplace in this room?   Yes ☐   No ☐

Fireplace construction is: Stone ☐   Brick ☐   Tile ☐   Metal ☐   Other _____

Fireplace enclosure is: Glass doors ☐   Screen ☐   None ☐   Other _____

Damper is: Maintained ☐   Repair ☐
(The damper is a metal plate inside the chimney necessary to close chimney flue.)

Fireplace or wood-burning stove are: Maintained ☐   Repair ☐

Notes: _____

This space is for an area photograph, notes, drawings, or for listing the contents and features of this area, such as furniture, art, TV, stereo, location of skylights, etc. For a complete listing of home contents, use the **Home Furnishings List** *in the* **Forms** *section at the back of the book.*

LIBRARY OR DEN

Dimensions: Length_____ Width_____ Height_____

The floor is: Wood ☐   Carpet ☐   Concrete ☐   Tile ☐   Brick ☐   Linoleum ☐
Other _____

The walls are: Plaster ☐   Drywall ☐   Wood ☐   Tile ☐   Wallpaper ☐
Other _____

The ceiling is: Plaster ☐   Drywall ☐   Wood ☐   Tile ☐   Wallpaper ☐
Other _____

Approximate
Floor color is:_____
Wall color is:_____
Ceiling color is:_____

Do you need to replace the floor? Are there any cracks, holes or squeaks?

Floor condition is: Maintained ☐   Repair ☐

Wall condition is: Maintained ☐   Repair ☐

Ceiling condition is: Maintained ☐   Repair ☐

Artificial lighting is: Maintained ☐   Repair ☐

Door condition is: Maintained ☐   Repair ☐

Is there a ceiling fan(s) *(Operating properly?)*   Yes ☐   No ☐

Is there fan lighting? *(Does it work? Pull chain or switch?)*   Yes ☐   No ☐

Any daylight sunshine? *(Can you see without artificial lighting?)*   Yes ☐   No ☐

Do the windows work properly? *(Is there any broken or cracked glass?)*   Yes ☐   No ☐

Total windows in this area: One ☐   Two ☐   Three ☐   Four ☐   More_____   None ☐

Total windows, screens or storms: Damaged_____   Missing_____

Window treatments: Drapes ☐   Shutters ☐   Blinds ☐   Verticals ☐   None ☐

Total electric outlets are:_____   **Total heat or air registers in this area are:**_____

Over-all Condition: Well-maintained ☐   Needs repair ☐

Is there a TV or cable connector? *(Do you need one in this room?)*   Yes ☐   No ☐

Is there a telephone connector? *(Do you need one in this room?)*   Yes ☐   No ☐

Is there a wood-burning stove in this room?   Yes ☐   No ☐

Is there a fireplace in this room?   Yes ☐   No ☐

Fireplace construction is: Stone ☐   Brick ☐   Tile ☐   Metal ☐   Other_____

Fireplace enclosure is: Glass doors ☐   Screen ☐   None ☐   Other_____

Damper is: Maintained ☐   Repair ☐
(The damper is a metal plate inside the chimney necessary to close chimney flue.)

Fireplace or wood-burning stove are: Maintained ☐   Repair ☐

Notes: _____

---

*This space is for an area photograph, notes, drawings, or for listing the contents and features of this area, such as furniture, art, TV, stereo, location of skylights, etc. For a complete listing of home contents, use the **Home Furnishings List** in the **Forms** section at the back of the book.*

LANAI OR ENCLOSED PORCH

Dimensions: Length_____ Width_____ Height_____

The floor is: Wood ☐ Carpet ☐ Concrete ☐ Tile ☐ Brick ☐ Linoleum ☐
Other_____

The walls are: Plaster ☐ Drywall ☐ Wood ☐ Tile ☐ Wallpaper ☐
Other_____

The ceiling is: Plaster ☐ Drywall ☐ Wood ☐ Tile ☐ Wallpaper ☐
Other_____

Approximate
Floor color is:_____
Wall color is:_____
Ceiling color is:_____

Do you need to replace the floor? Are there any cracks, holes or squeaks?

Floor condition is: Maintained ☐ Repair ☐

Wall condition is: Maintained ☐ Repair ☐

Ceiling condition is: Maintained ☐ Repair ☐

Artificial lighting is: Maintained ☐ Repair ☐

Door condition is: Maintained ☐ Repair ☐

Is there a ceiling fan(s) *(Operating properly?)* Yes ☐ No ☐

Is there fan lighting? *(Does it work? Pull chain or switch?)* Yes ☐ No ☐

Any daylight sunshine? *(Can you see without artificial lighting?)* Yes ☐ No ☐

Do the windows work properly? *(Is there any broken or cracked glass?)* Yes ☐ No ☐

Total windows in this area: One ☐ Two ☐ Three ☐ Four ☐ More_____ None ☐

Total windows, screens or storms: Damaged_____ Missing_____

Window treatments: Drapes ☐ Shutters ☐ Blinds ☐ Verticals ☐ None ☐

Total electric outlets are:_____ **Total heat or air registers in this area are:_____**

Over-all Condition: Well-maintained ☐ Needs repair ☐

Is there a TV or cable connector? *(Do you need one in this room?)*   Yes ☐   No ☐

Is there a telephone connector? *(Do you need one in this room?)*   Yes ☐   No ☐

Is there a wood-burning stove in this room?   Yes ☐   No ☐

Is there a fireplace in this room?   Yes ☐   No ☐

Fireplace construction is: Stone ☐   Brick ☐   Tile ☐   Metal ☐   Other _____

Fireplace enclosure is: Glass doors ☐   Screen ☐   None ☐   Other _____

Damper is: Maintained ☐   Repair ☐
(The damper is a metal plate inside the chimney necessary to close chimney flue.)

Fireplace or wood-burning stove are: Maintained ☐   Repair ☐

Notes: _____

---

*This space is for an area photograph, notes, drawings, or for listing the contents and features of this area, such as furniture, art, TV, stereo, location of skylights, etc. For a complete listing of home contents, use the **Home Furnishings List** in the **Forms** section at the back of the book.*

MASTER BEDROOM

Dimensions: Length_____ Width_____ Height_____

The floor is: Wood ☐   Carpet ☐   Concrete ☐   Tile ☐   Brick ☐   Linoleum ☐
Other_____

The walls are: Plaster ☐   Drywall ☐   Wood ☐   Tile ☐   Wallpaper ☐
Other_____

The ceiling is: Plaster ☐   Drywall ☐   Wood ☐   Tile ☐   Wallpaper ☐
Other_____

Approximate   Floor color is:_____

Wall color is:_____

Ceiling color is:_____

Do you need to replace the floor? Are there any cracks, holes or squeaks?

Floor condition is: Maintained ☐   Repair ☐

Wall condition is: Maintained ☐   Repair ☐

Ceiling condition is: Maintained ☐   Repair ☐

Artificial lighting is: Maintained ☐   Repair ☐

Door condition is: Maintained ☐   Repair ☐

Is there a ceiling fan(s)? *(Operating properly?)*   Yes ☐   No ☐

Is there fan lighting? *(Does it work? Pull chain or switch?)*   Yes ☐   No ☐

Any daylight sunshine? *(Can you see without artificial lighting?)*   Yes ☐   No ☐

Do the windows work properly? *(Is there any broken or cracked glass?)*   Yes ☐   No ☐

Total windows in this area: One ☐   Two ☐   Three ☐   Four ☐   More_____   None ☐

Total windows, screens or storms: Damaged_____   Missing_____

Window treatments: Drapes ☐   Shutters ☐   Blinds ☐   Verticals ☐   None ☐

Total electric outlets are:_____   **Total heat or air registers in this area are:**_____

Over-all Condition: Well-maintained ☐   Needs repair ☐

Is there a clothes closet? *(Do you have room for storage?)*   Yes ☐   No ☐

Is there a TV or cable connector? *(Do you need one in this room?)*   Yes ☐   No ☐

Is there a telephone connector? *(Do you need one in this room?)*   Yes ☐   No ☐

Is there a wood-burning stove in this room?   Yes ☐   No ☐

Is there a fireplace in this room?   Yes ☐   No ☐

Fireplace construction is: Stone ☐   Brick ☐   Tile ☐   Metal ☐   Other_____

Fireplace enclosure is: Glass doors ☐   Screen ☐   None ☐   Other_____

Damper is: Maintained ☐   Repair ☐
(The damper is a metal plate inside the chimney necessary to close chimney flue.)

Fireplace or wood-burning stove are: Maintained ☐   Repair ☐

Notes: _____

---

*This space is for an area photograph, notes, drawings, or for listing the contents and features of this area, such as furniture, art, TV, stereo, location of skylights, etc. For a complete listing of home contents, use the **Home Furnishings List** in the **Forms** section at the back of the book.*

BEDROOM NUMBER TWO

Dimensions: Length_____ Width_____ Height_____

The floor is: Wood ☐ Carpet ☐ Concrete ☐ Tile ☐ Brick ☐ Linoleum ☐
Other _____

The walls are: Plaster ☐ Drywall ☐ Wood ☐ Tile ☐ Wallpaper ☐
Other _____

The ceiling is: Plaster ☐ Drywall ☐ Wood ☐ Tile ☐ Wallpaper ☐
Other _____

Approximate
Floor color is:_____
Wall color is:_____
Ceiling color is:_____

Do you need to replace the floor? Are there any cracks, holes or squeaks?

Floor condition is: Maintained ☐ Repair ☐

Wall condition is: Maintained ☐ Repair ☐

Ceiling condition is: Maintained ☐ Repair ☐

Artificial lighting is: Maintained ☐ Repair ☐

Door condition is: Maintained ☐ Repair ☐

Is there a ceiling fan(s)? *(Operating properly?)* Yes ☐ No ☐

Is there fan lighting? *(Does it work? Pull chain or switch?)* Yes ☐ No ☐

Any daylight sunshine? *(Can you see without artificial lighting?)* Yes ☐ No ☐

Do the windows work properly? *(Is there any broken or cracked glass?)* Yes ☐ No ☐

Total windows in this area: One ☐ Two ☐ Three ☐ Four ☐ More_____ None ☐

Total windows, screens or storms: Damaged_____ Missing_____

Window treatments: Drapes ☐ Shutters ☐ Blinds ☐ Verticals ☐ None ☐

Total electric outlets are:_____ **Total heat or air registers in this area are:**_____

Over-all Condition: Well-maintained ☐ Needs repair ☐

Is there a clothes closet? *(Do you have room for storage?)*   Yes ☐   No ☐

Is there a TV or cable connector? *(Do you need one in this room?)*   Yes ☐   No ☐

Is there a telephone connector? *(Do you need one in this room?)*   Yes ☐   No ☐

Is there a wood-burning stove in this room?   Yes ☐   No ☐

Is there a fireplace in this room?   Yes ☐   No ☐

Fireplace construction is: Stone ☐   Brick ☐   Tile ☐   Metal ☐   Other _____

Fireplace enclosure is: Glass doors ☐   Screen ☐   None ☐   Other _____

Damper is: Maintained ☐   Repair ☐
(The damper is a metal plate inside the chimney necessary to close chimney flue.)

Fireplace or wood-burning stove are: Maintained ☐   Repair ☐

Notes: _____

---

*This space is for an area photograph, notes, drawings, or for listing the contents and features of this area, such as furniture, art, TV, stereo, location of skylights, etc. For a complete listing of home contents, use the **Home Furnishings List** in the **Forms** section at the back of the book.*

BEDROOM NUMBER THREE

Dimensions: Length_____ Width_____ Height_____

The floor is: Wood ☐ Carpet ☐ Concrete ☐ Tile ☐ Brick ☐ Linoleum ☐
Other _____

The walls are: Plaster ☐ Drywall ☐ Wood ☐ Tile ☐ Wallpaper ☐
Other _____

The ceiling is: Plaster ☐ Drywall ☐ Wood ☐ Tile ☐ Wallpaper ☐
Other _____

Approximate
Floor color is:_____
Wall color is:_____
Ceiling color is:_____

Do you need to replace the floor? Are there any cracks, holes or squeaks?

Floor condition is:	Maintained ☐	Repair ☐
Wall condition is:	Maintained ☐	Repair ☐
Ceiling condition is:	Maintained ☐	Repair ☐
Artificial lighting is:	Maintained ☐	Repair ☐
Door condition is:	Maintained ☐	Repair ☐
Is there a ceiling fan(s)? *(Operating properly?)*	Yes ☐	No ☐
Is there fan lighting? *(Does it work? Pull chain or switch?)*	Yes ☐	No ☐
Any daylight sunshine? *(Can you see without artificial lighting?)*	Yes ☐	No ☐
Do the windows work properly? *(Is there any broken or cracked glass?)*	Yes ☐	No ☐

Total windows in this area: One ☐ Two ☐ Three ☐ Four ☐ More_____ None ☐

Total windows, screens or storms: Damaged_____ Missing_____

Window treatments: Drapes ☐ Shutters ☐ Blinds ☐ Verticals ☐ None ☐

Total electric outlets are:_____ **Total heat or air registers in this area are:**_____

Over-all Condition: Well-maintained ☐ Needs repair ☐

Is there a clothes closet? *(Do you have room for storage?)*   Yes ☐   No ☐

Is there a TV or cable connector? *(Do you need one in this room?)*   Yes ☐   No ☐

Is there a telephone connector? *(Do you need one in this room?)*   Yes ☐   No ☐

Is there a wood-burning stove in this room?   Yes ☐   No ☐

Is there a fireplace in this room?   Yes ☐   No ☐

Fireplace construction is: Stone ☐   Brick ☐   Tile ☐   Metal ☐   Other _____

Fireplace enclosure is: Glass doors ☐   Screen ☐   None ☐   Other _____

Damper is: Maintained ☐   Repair ☐
(The damper is a metal plate inside the chimney necessary to close chimney flue.)

Fireplace or wood-burning stove are: Maintained ☐   Repair ☐

Notes: _____

---

*This space is for an area photograph, notes, drawings, or for listing the contents and features of this area, such as furniture, art, TV, stereo, location of skylights, etc. For a complete listing of home contents, use the **Home Furnishings List** in the **Forms** section at the back of the book.*

BEDROOM NUMBER FOUR

Dimensions: Length_____ Width_____ Height_____

The floor is: Wood ☐   Carpet ☐   Concrete ☐   Tile ☐   Brick ☐   Linoleum ☐
Other _____

The walls are: Plaster ☐   Drywall ☐   Wood ☐   Tile ☐   Wallpaper ☐
Other _____

The ceiling is: Plaster ☐   Drywall ☐   Wood ☐   Tile ☐   Wallpaper ☐
Other _____

<u>Approximate</u>
Floor color is:_____
Wall color is:_____
Ceiling color is:_____

Do you need to replace the floor? Are there any cracks, holes or squeaks?

Floor condition is:	Maintained ☐	Repair ☐
Wall condition is:	Maintained ☐	Repair ☐
Ceiling condition is:	Maintained ☐	Repair ☐
Artificial lighting is:	Maintained ☐	Repair ☐
Door condition is:	Maintained ☐	Repair ☐
Is there a ceiling fan(s)? *(Operating properly?)*	Yes ☐	No ☐
Is there fan lighting? *(Does it work? Pull chain or switch?)*	Yes ☐	No ☐
Any daylight sunshine? *(Can you see without artificial lighting?)*	Yes ☐	No ☐
Do the windows work properly? *(Is there any broken or cracked glass?)*	Yes ☐	No ☐

Total windows in this area: One ☐   Two ☐   Three ☐   Four ☐   More_____   None ☐

Total windows, screens or storms: Damaged_____   Missing_____

Window treatments: Drapes ☐   Shutters ☐   Blinds ☐   Verticals ☐   None ☐

Total electric outlets are:_____   Total heat or air registers in this area are:_____

Over-all Condition: Well-maintained ☐   Needs repair ☐

Is there a clothes closet? *(Do you have room for storage?)*   Yes ☐   No ☐

Is there a TV or cable connector? *(Do you need one in this room?)*   Yes ☐   No ☐

Is there a telephone connector? *(Do you need one in this room?)*   Yes ☐   No ☐

Is there a wood-burning stove in this room?   Yes ☐   No ☐

Is there a fireplace in this room?   Yes ☐   No ☐

Fireplace construction is: Stone ☐   Brick ☐   Tile ☐   Metal ☐   Other_____

Fireplace enclosure is: Glass doors ☐   Screen ☐   None ☐   Other_____

Damper is: Maintained ☐   Repair ☐
(The damper is a metal plate inside the chimney necessary to close chimney flue.)

Fireplace or wood-burning stove are: Maintained ☐   Repair ☐

Notes: _____

---

*This space is for an area photograph, notes, drawings, or for listing the contents and features of this area, such as furniture, art, TV, stereo, location of skylights, etc. For a complete listing of home contents, use the **Home Furnishings List** in the **Forms** section at the back of the book.*

MASTER BATHROOM

Dimensions:	Length_____		Width_____		Height_____	
The floor is:	Wood ☐	Carpet ☐	Concrete ☐	Tile ☐	Brick ☐	Linoleum ☐
	Other _____					
The walls are:	Plaster ☐	Drywall ☐	Wood ☐	Tile ☐	Wallpaper ☐	
	Other _____					
The ceiling is:	Plaster ☐	Drywall ☐	Wood ☐	Tile ☐	Wallpaper ☐	
	Other _____					
Cabinets are:	Wood ☐		Metal ☐		Plastic Laminate ☐	
	Other _____					
Counter top is:	Wood ☐	Metal ☐		Plastic Laminate ☐		Tile ☐
	Other _____					
Tub or shower walls are:	Wood ☐	Metal ☐		Plastic Laminate ☐		Tile ☐
	Other _____					

Approximate Floor color is:_____

Wall color is:_____

Ceiling color is:_____

Do you need to replace the floor? Are there any cracks, holes or squeaks?

Floor condition is:	Maintained ☐	Repair ☐
Wall condition is:	Maintained ☐	Repair ☐
Ceiling condition is:	Maintained ☐	Repair ☐
Bathroom door condition is:	Maintained ☐	Repair ☐
Cabinet condition is:	Maintained ☐	Repair ☐
Counter top condition is:	Maintained ☐	Repair ☐
Sink and tub condition is:	Maintained ☐	Repair ☐
Artificial lighting condition is:	Maintained ☐	Repair ☐

Do the cabinet door hinges work? *(All the same style? Any loose?)*	Yes ☐	No ☐
Do the cabinet drawers work? *(Sliding guides work properly?)*	Yes ☐	No ☐
Are outlets on GFCIs? *(Better to be safe than sorry.)*	Yes ☐	No ☐
Is there a linen closet? *(Do you have enough room for storage?)*	Yes ☐	No ☐
Is the toilet firm to the floor? *(If "no," seal may need repairing.)*	Yes ☐	No ☐
Is the toilet seat broken or loose? *(Does the seat need replacement?)*	Yes ☐	No ☐

Is there a bidet installed? *(A European wash basin.)*	Yes ☐	No ☐
Is there hot & cold water? *(Check under the sink for leaks.)*	Yes ☐	No ☐
Do the sink, toilet, tub or bidet leak? *(Check for water spots.)*	Yes ☐	No ☐
Is the water pressure okay? *(Approximately 4 gallons per minute.)*	Yes ☐	No ☐
Is there a ceiling fan(s)? *(Operating properly?)*	Yes ☐	No ☐
Is there fan lighting? *(Does it work? Pull chain or switch?)*	Yes ☐	No ☐
Any daylight sunshine? *(Can you see without artificial lighting?)*	Yes ☐	No ☐
Do the windows work properly? *(Is there any broken or cracked glass?)*	Yes ☐	No ☐

Total windows in this area: One ☐ Two ☐ Three ☐ Four ☐ More_____ None ☐

Total windows, screens or storms: Damaged_____ Missing_____

Window treatments: Drapes ☐ Shutters ☐ Blinds ☐ Verticals ☐ None ☐

Total electric outlets are:_____ **Total heat or air registers in this area are:**_____

Over-all Condition: Well-maintained ☐ Needs repair ☐

Notes: _____

---

*This space is for an area photograph, notes, drawings, or for listing the contents and features of this area, such as furniture, art, TV, stereo, location of skylights, etc. For a complete listing of home contents, use the **Home Furnishings List** in the **Forms** section at the back of the book.*

BATHROOM NUMBER TWO

Dimensions: Length_____ Width_____ Height_____

The floor is: Wood ☐ Carpet ☐ Concrete ☐ Tile ☐ Brick ☐ Linoleum ☐
Other _____

The walls are: Plaster ☐ Drywall ☐ Wood ☐ Tile ☐ Wallpaper ☐
Other _____

The ceiling is: Plaster ☐ Drywall ☐ Wood ☐ Tile ☐ Wallpaper ☐
Other _____

Cabinets are: Wood ☐ Metal ☐ Plastic Laminate ☐
Other _____

Counter top is: Wood ☐ Metal ☐ Plastic Laminate ☐ Tile ☐
Other _____

Tub or shower walls are: Wood ☐ Metal ☐ Plastic Laminate ☐ Tile ☐
Other _____

Approximate
Floor color is:_____
Wall color is:_____
Ceiling color is:_____

Do you need to replace the floor? Are there any cracks, holes or squeaks?

Floor condition is:	Maintained ☐	Repair ☐
Wall condition is:	Maintained ☐	Repair ☐
Ceiling condition is:	Maintained ☐	Repair ☐
Bathroom door condition is:	Maintained ☐	Repair ☐
Cabinet condition is:	Maintained ☐	Repair ☐
Counter top condition is:	Maintained ☐	Repair ☐
Sink and tub condition is:	Maintained ☐	Repair ☐
Artificial lighting condition is:	Maintained ☐	Repair ☐
Do the cabinet door hinges work? *(All the same style? Any loose?)*	Yes ☐	No ☐
Do the cabinet drawers work? *(Sliding guides work properly?)*	Yes ☐	No ☐
Are outlets on GFCIs? *(Better to be safe than sorry.)*	Yes ☐	No ☐
Is there a linen closet? *(Do you have enough room for storage?)*	Yes ☐	No ☐
Is the toilet firm to the floor? *(If "no," seal may need repairing.)*	Yes ☐	No ☐
Is the toilet seat broken or loose? *(Does the seat need replacement?)*	Yes ☐	No ☐

Is there a bidet installed? *(A European wash basin.)*	Yes ☐	No ☐
Is there hot & cold water? *(Check under the sink for leaks.)*	Yes ☐	No ☐
Do the sink, toilet, tub or bidet leak? *(Check for water spots.)*	Yes ☐	No ☐
Is the water pressure okay? *(Approximately 4 gallons per minute.)*	Yes ☐	No ☐
Is there a ceiling fan(s)? *(Operating properly?)*	Yes ☐	No ☐
Is there fan lighting? *(Does it work? Pull chain or switch?)*	Yes ☐	No ☐
Any daylight sunshine? *(Can you see without artificial lighting?)*	Yes ☐	No ☐
Do the windows work properly? *(Is there any broken or cracked glass?)*	Yes ☐	No ☐

Total windows in this area: One ☐   Two ☐   Three ☐   Four ☐   More_____   None ☐

Total windows, screens or storms: Damaged_____   Missing_____

Window treatments: Drapes ☐   Shutters ☐   Blinds ☐   Verticals ☐   None ☐

Total electric outlets are:_____   **Total heat or air registers in this area are:**_____

Over-all Condition: Well-maintained ☐   Needs repair ☐

Notes: _____

---

*This space is for an area photograph, notes, drawings, or for listing the contents and features of this area, such as furniture, art, TV, stereo, location of skylights, etc. For a complete listing of home contents, use the **Home Furnishings List** in the **Forms** section at the back of the book.*

BATHROOM NUMBER THREE

Dimensions:	Length_____		Width_____		Height_____	
The floor is:	Wood ☐	Carpet ☐	Concrete ☐	Tile ☐	Brick ☐	Linoleum ☐
	Other _____					
The walls are:	Plaster ☐	Drywall ☐	Wood ☐	Tile ☐		Wallpaper ☐
	Other _____					
The ceiling is:	Plaster ☐	Drywall ☐	Wood ☐	Tile ☐		Wallpaper ☐
	Other _____					
Cabinets are:	Wood ☐		Metal ☐			Plastic Laminate ☐
	Other _____					
Counter top is:	Wood ☐	Metal ☐		Plastic Laminate ☐		Tile ☐
	Other _____					
Tub or shower walls are:	Wood ☐	Metal ☐		Plastic Laminate ☐		Tile ☐
	Other _____					

Approximate Floor color is:_____

Wall color is:_____

Ceiling color is:_____

Do you need to replace the floor? Are there any cracks, holes or squeaks?

Floor condition is:	Maintained ☐	Repair ☐
Wall condition is:	Maintained ☐	Repair ☐
Ceiling condition is:	Maintained ☐	Repair ☐
Bathroom door condition is:	Maintained ☐	Repair ☐
Cabinet condition is:	Maintained ☐	Repair ☐
Counter top condition is:	Maintained ☐	Repair ☐
Sink and tub condition is:	Maintained ☐	Repair ☐
Artificial lighting condition is:	Maintained ☐	Repair ☐
Do the cabinet door hinges work? *(All the same style? Any loose?)*	Yes ☐	No ☐
Do the cabinet drawers work? *(Sliding guides work properly?)*	Yes ☐	No ☐
Are outlets on GFCIs? *(Better to be safe than sorry.)*	Yes ☐	No ☐
Is there a linen closet? *(Do you have enough room for storage?)*	Yes ☐	No ☐
Is the toilet firm to the floor? *(If "no," seal may need repairing.)*	Yes ☐	No ☐
Is the toilet seat broken or loose? *(Does the seat need replacement?)*	Yes ☐	No ☐

Is there a bidet installed? *(A European wash basin.)*	Yes ☐	No ☐
Is there hot & cold water? *(Check under the sink for leaks.)*	Yes ☐	No ☐
Do the sink, toilet, tub or bidet leak? *(Check for water spots.)*	Yes ☐	No ☐
Is the water pressure okay? *(Approximately 4 gallons per minute.)*	Yes ☐	No ☐
Is there a ceiling fan(s)? *(Operating properly?)*	Yes ☐	No ☐
Is there fan lighting? *(Does it work? Pull chain or switch?)*	Yes ☐	No ☐
Any daylight sunshine? *(Can you see without artificial lighting?)*	Yes ☐	No ☐
Do the windows work properly? *(Is there any broken or cracked glass?)*	Yes ☐	No ☐

Total windows in this area: One ☐ Two ☐ Three ☐ Four ☐ More_____ None ☐

Total windows, screens or storms: Damaged_____ Missing_____

Window treatments: Drapes ☐ Shutters ☐ Blinds ☐ Verticals ☐ None ☐

Total electric outlets are:_____ **Total heat or air registers in this area are:**_____

Over-all Condition: Well-maintained ☐ Needs repair ☐

Notes: _____

---

*This space is for an area photograph, notes, drawings, or for listing the contents and features of this area, such as furniture, art, TV, stereo, location of skylights, etc. For a complete listing of home contents, use the **Home Furnishings List** in the **Forms** section at the back of the book.*

HALLWAY

Dimensions:	Length_____		Width_____		Height_____	
The floor is:	Wood ☐	Carpet ☐	Concrete ☐	Tile ☐	Brick ☐	Linoleum ☐
	Other _____					
The walls are:	Plaster ☐	Drywall ☐	Wood ☐	Tile ☐	Wallpaper ☐	
	Other _____					
The ceiling is:	Plaster ☐	Drywall ☐	Wood ☐	Tile ☐	Wallpaper ☐	
	Other _____					

Approximate   Floor color is:_____

Wall color is:_____

Ceiling color is:_____

Do you need to replace the floor? Are there any cracks, holes or squeaks?

Floor condition is: Maintained ☐   Repair ☐

Wall condition is: Maintained ☐   Repair ☐

Ceiling condition is: Maintained ☐   Repair ☐

Door condition is: Maintained ☐   Repair ☐

Any hallway lighting? *(Is there a light switch at both ends of the hall?)*   Yes ☐   No ☐

Any daylight sunshine? *(Can you see without artificial lighting?)*   Yes ☐   No ☐

Is there an electric outlet? *(Useful for night light or vacuum cleaner.)*   Yes ☐   No ☐

Is there a smoke detector installed? *(Battery or electric?)*   Yes ☐   No ☐

Do you have an intercom system throughout the house?   Yes ☐   No ☐

Is there a closet? *(Do you have room for storage?)*   Yes ☐   No ☐

Any cold air returns? *(Returns air to the central heat & air system.)*   Yes ☐   No ☐

Is an alarm system installed and working properly?   Yes ☐   No ☐

Over-all Condition: Well-maintained ☐   Needs repair ☐

NOTE: When purchasing a home, never ask questions concerning the operation of the alarm system. Wait until you close and the house is yours, then ask.

STAIRWAY

The steps are:	Wood ☐ Carpet ☐ Concrete ☐ Tile ☐ Brick ☐ Linoleum ☐
	Other _____

The walls are:	Plaster ☐ Drywall ☐ Wood ☐ Tile ☐ Wallpaper ☐
	Other _____

The ceiling is:	Plaster ☐ Drywall ☐ Wood ☐ Tile ☐ Wallpaper ☐
	Other _____

Approximate

Floor color is: _____

Wall color is: _____

Ceiling color is: _____

Do you need to replace the stairs? Are there any cracks, holes or squeaks?

Stair condition is:	Maintained ☐	Repair ☐
Wall condition is:	Maintained ☐	Repair ☐
Ceiling condition is:	Maintained ☐	Repair ☐
Door condition is:	Maintained ☐	Repair ☐

Is there a hand rail? *(Always think safety first)*   Yes ☐   No ☐

Any stairway lights? *(Is there a light switch at both ends of the stairs?)*   Yes ☐   No ☐

Any daylight sunshine? *(Can you see without artificial lighting?)*   Yes ☐   No ☐

Is there an electric outlet? *(Useful for night light or vacuum cleaner.)*   Yes ☐   No ☐

Is there a smoke detector installed? *(Battery or electric?)*   Yes ☐   No ☐

Any cold air returns? *(Returns air to the central heat & air system.)*   Yes ☐   No ☐

Over-all Condition: Well-maintained ☐   Needs repair ☐

Notes: _____

BASEMENT

Dimensions: Length_____ Width_____ Height_____

The stairs are: Wood ☐ Carpet ☐ Concrete ☐ Tile ☐ Brick ☐ Linoleum ☐
Other _____

The floor is: Wood ☐ Carpet ☐ Concrete ☐ Tile ☐ Brick ☐ Linoleum ☐
Other _____

The walls are: Plaster ☐ Drywall ☐ Wood ☐ Tile ☐ Wallpaper ☐
Other _____

The ceiling is: Plaster ☐ Drywall ☐ Wood ☐ Tile ☐ Wallpaper ☐
Other _____

Approximate
Floor color is:_____
Wall color is:_____
Ceiling color is:_____

Do you need to replace the floor? Are there any cracks, holes or squeaks?

Stair condition is:	Maintained ☐	Repair ☐
Floor condition is:	Maintained ☐	Repair ☐
Wall condition is:	Maintained ☐	Repair ☐
Ceiling condition is:	Maintained ☐	Repair ☐
Door condition is:	Maintained ☐	Repair ☐
Artificial lighting is:	Maintained ☐	Repair ☐

Is there a hand rail? *(Always think safety first.)* Yes ☐ No ☐

Any stairway lights? *(Is there a light switch at both ends of the stairs?)* Yes ☐ No ☐

Is there an electric outlet? *(Useful for night light or vacuum cleaner.)* Yes ☐ No ☐

Any sump pump(s)? *(Used to remove unwanted underground water.)* Yes ☐ No ☐

Has the basement ever flooded? Yes ☐ No ☐
(Check for water marks on walls. Are there enough floor drains?)

Is there any dampness? *(If "yes," check for mildew and dry rot.)* Yes ☐ No ☐

Is there a fire extinguisher? *(ABC type dry-chemical for all fires.)* Yes ☐ No ☐

Is there a smoke detector installed? *(Battery or electric?)* Yes ☐ No ☐

Is there an intercom system throughout the house? Yes ☐ No ☐

Is there a TV or cable connector? *(Do you need one in this room?)* Yes ☐ No ☐

Is there a telephone connector? *(Do you need one in this room?)*	Yes ☐	No ☐
Is there a ceiling fan(s)? *(Operating properly?)*	Yes ☐	No ☐
Is there fan lighting? *(Does it work? Pull chain or switch?)*	Yes ☐	No ☐
Any daylight sunshine? *(Can you see without artificial lighting?)*	Yes ☐	No ☐
Do the windows work properly? *(Is there any broken or cracked glass?)*	Yes ☐	No ☐

Total windows in this area: One ☐   Two ☐   Three ☐   Four ☐   More _____   None ☐

Total windows, screens or storms: Damaged _____   Missing _____

Window treatments: Drapes ☐   Shutters ☐   Blinds ☐   Verticals ☐   None ☐

Total electric outlets are: _____   **Total heat or air registers in this area are:** _____

Over-all Condition: Well-maintained ☐   Needs repair ☐

Is there a wood-burning stove in this room?   Yes ☐   No ☐

Is there a fireplace in this room?   Yes ☐   No ☐

Fireplace construction is: Stone ☐   Brick ☐   Tile ☐   Metal ☐   Other _____

Fireplace enclosure is: Glass doors ☐   Screen ☐   None ☐   Other _____

Damper is: Maintained ☐   Repair ☐
(The damper is a metal plate inside the chimney necessary to close chimney flue.)

Fireplace or wood-burning stove are: Maintained ☐   Repair ☐

Notes: _____

---

*This space is for an area photograph, notes, drawings, or for listing the contents and features of this area, such as furniture, art, TV, stereo, location of skylights, etc. For a complete listing of home contents, use the **Home Furnishings List** in the **Forms** section at the back of the book.*

LAUNDRY ROOM

Dimensions: Length_____ Width_____ Height_____

The floor is: Wood ☐ Carpet ☐ Concrete ☐ Tile ☐ Brick ☐ Linoleum ☐
Other _____

The walls are: Plaster ☐ Drywall ☐ Wood ☐ Tile ☐ Wallpaper ☐
Other _____

The ceiling is: Plaster ☐ Drywall ☐ Wood ☐ Tile ☐ Wallpaper ☐
Other _____

Approximate   Floor color is:_____

Wall color is:_____

Ceiling color is:_____

Do you need to replace the floor? Are there any cracks, holes or squeaks?

Floor condition is:	Maintained ☐	Repair ☐
Wall condition is:	Maintained ☐	Repair ☐
Ceiling condition is:	Maintained ☐	Repair ☐
Door condition is:	Maintained ☐	Repair ☐
Artificial lighting is:	Maintained ☐	Repair ☐
Will the washer and dryer remain? *(Do they work properly?)*	Yes ☐	No ☐
Do you have the owner's manual? *(Useful for part replacement.)*	Yes ☐	No ☐
Are there separate hot & cold water lines for a washing machine?	Yes ☐	No ☐
Is the water pressure okay? *(Approximately 4 gallons per minute.)*	Yes ☐	No ☐
Is the dryer vent installed? *(Is it vented to the outside?)*	Yes ☐	No ☐

The dryer uses: Natural gas ☐ LP gas ☐ Electric ☐

Is there a gas main shut-off valve?   Yes ☐ No ☐

The location of the gas-line shut-off valve for the dryer is:_____

_____

Laundry Tub: *(Is it One or Two compartments?)* Plastic ☐ Metal ☐ Cement ☐ Wood ☐

Is there a TV or cable connector? *(Do you need one in this room?)* Yes ☐ No ☐

Is there a telephone connector? *(Do you need one in this room?)* Yes ☐ No ☐

Is there a ceiling fan(s)? *(Operating properly?)* Yes ☐ No ☐

Is there fan lighting? *(Does it work? Pull chain or switch?)*   Yes ☐   No ☐

Any daylight sunshine? *(Can you see without artificial lighting?)*   Yes ☐   No ☐

Do the windows work properly? *(Is there any broken or cracked glass?)*   Yes ☐   No ☐

Are the outlets on GFCIs? *(Better to be safe than sorry.)*   Yes ☐   No ☐

Total windows in this area: One ☐   Two ☐   Three ☐   Four ☐   More_____   None ☐

Total windows, screens or storms: Damaged_____   Missing_____

Window treatments: Drapes ☐   Shutters ☐   Blinds ☐   Verticals ☐   None ☐

Total electric outlets are:_____   **Total heat or air registers in this area are:**_____

Over-all Condition: Well-maintained ☐   Needs repair ☐

Notes: _____

Notes:

*This space is for an area photograph, notes, drawings, or for listing the contents and features of this area, such as furniture, art, TV, stereo, location of skylights, etc. For a complete listing of home contents, use the **Home Furnishings List** in the **Forms** section at the back of the book.*

ATTACHED GARAGE INTERIOR

Dimensions: Length_____ Width_____ Height_____

The floor is: Concrete ☐ Tile ☐ Brick ☐ Linoleum ☐ Asphalt ☐ Painted ☐
Other _____

The walls are: Plaster ☐ Drywall ☐ Wood ☐ Tile ☐ Wallpaper ☐ Unfinished ☐
Other _____

The ceiling is: Plaster ☐ Drywall ☐ Wood ☐ Tile ☐ Wallpaper ☐ Unfinished ☐
Other _____

The total car capacity is:_____

Approximate

Floor color is:_____

Wall color is:_____

Ceiling color is:_____

Do you need to replace the floor? Are there any cracks, holes or squeaks?

Floor condition is:	Maintained ☐	Repair ☐
Wall condition is:	Maintained ☐	Repair ☐
Ceiling condition is:	Maintained ☐	Repair ☐
Artificial lighting is:	Maintained ☐	Repair ☐

Is there a fire extinguisher? *(ABC type dry-chemical for all fires.)* Yes ☐ No ☐

Any daylight sunshine? *(Can you see without artificial lighting?)* Yes ☐ No ☐

Do the windows work properly? *(Is there any broken or cracked glass?)* Yes ☐ No ☐

Total windows in this area: One ☐ Two ☐ Three ☐ Four ☐ More_____ None ☐

Total windows, screens or storms: Damaged_____ Missing_____

Window treatments: Drapes ☐ Shutters ☐ Blinds ☐ Verticals ☐ None ☐

Total electric outlets are:_____ **Total heat or air registers in this area are:**_____

The total inches of insulation are: Walls_____ Ceiling_____ None ☐

Over-all Condition: Well-maintained ☐ Needs repair ☐

Note: Is there enough room for storing your lawn furniture, storm windows, snowmobiles, bicycles, motorcycles, riding mower, and do you have enough room for a work bench?

ATTACHED GARAGE SERVICE DOOR

Construction is: Wood ☐   Steel ☐   Aluminum ☐   Other _____

Is there a window? *(Will the window open for ventilation?)*   Yes ☐   No ☐

Do the doors and lock(s) work properly?   Yes ☐   No ☐

Over-all Condition: Well-maintained ☐   Needs repair ☐

ATTACHED GARAGE DOOR

Door dimensions: Height _____   Width _____

Construction is: Wood ☐   Steel ☐   Aluminum ☐   Vinyl ☐   Fiberglass ☐
Other _____

Door swing direction is: Overhead ☐   Side-hinged ☐   Other _____

Is there a weather strip attached to the bottom of the garage door to produce a weather-tight seal and keep animals out?   Yes ☐   No ☐

Will the garage door lock?   Yes ☐   No ☐

Any windows on the garage door? *(Is there any broken or cracked glass?)*   Yes ☐   No ☐

Is there an electric garage-door opener?   Yes ☐   No ☐

Do you have the door-opener remote controls?   Yes ☐   No ☐

The manufacturer's name is: _____

The style or type of door is: _____

Over-all Condition: Well-maintained ☐   Needs repair ☐

NOTE: Remember to take possession of the garage-door remote controls at the house closing.

Notes: _____

 **_Notes:_**

---

*This space is for an area photograph, notes, drawings, or for listing the contents and features of this area, such as furniture, art, TV, stereo, location of skylights, etc. For a complete listing of home contents, use the **Home Furnishings List** in the **Forms** section at the back of the book.*

DETACHED GARAGE ROOF

DANGER: <u>Never climb on the roof.</u> <u>Leave this to the professionals.</u> You can inspect the roof from the ground if you stand back and look carefully. If you cannot see the roof's details very well, use a telescope or binoculars.

Construction is: Wood ☐ Asphalt ☐ Shingle ☐ Asbestos ☐ Cement ☐ Slate ☐ Tile ☐ Metal ☐ Other _____

Estimated age of roof in:	Years_____	Months_____
Have you recently repaired the roof?	Yes ☐	No ☐
Is there roof ventilation? *(Keeps the attic cool and prolongs roof life)*	Yes ☐	No ☐
Are there any tree limbs on the roof? *(Avoid roof damage.)*	Yes ☐	No ☐
Does the roof sag or bow? *(Roof may be weak. Contact a roofer.)*	Yes ☐	No ☐
Are there any roof leaks? *(Check inside ceilings for water leaks.)*	Yes ☐	No ☐
Flashing condition is: *(Prevents water leaks.)*	Maintained ☐	Repair ☐
Seals around vents are: *(Prevents water leaks.)*	Maintained ☐	Repair ☐
Over-all Condition:	Well-maintained ☐	Needs repair ☐

Check here if the roof is snow covered and could not be examined. ☐

DETACHED GARAGE EXTERIOR

Dimensions: Length_____ Width_____ Height_____

Your lot survey can help you with precise home exterior & lot dimensions.

Construction is: Brick ☐ Aluminum ☐ Vinyl ☐ Wood ☐ Shingle ☐ Asbestos ☐ Block ☐ Stucco ☐ Stone ☐ Other_____

Paint and caulking is:	Maintained ☐	Repair ☐
Gutters & downspouts are:	Maintained ☐	Repair ☐

Total faucet bibs are:_____ **Total electrical outlets (GFCIs) are:**_____

Over-all Condition: Well-maintained ☐ Needs repair ☐

DETACHED GARAGE INTERIOR

Dimensions: Length_____ Width_____ Height_____

The floor is: Concrete ☐ Tile ☐ Brick ☐ Linoleum ☐ Asphalt ☐ Painted ☐
Other _____

The walls are: Plaster ☐ Drywall ☐ Wood ☐ Tile ☐ Wallpaper ☐ Unfinished ☐
Other _____

The ceiling is: Plaster ☐ Drywall ☐ Wood ☐ Tile ☐ Wallpaper ☐ Unfinished ☐
Other _____

The total car capacity is:_____

<u>**Approximate**</u> Floor color is:_____

Wall color is:_____

Ceiling color is:_____

Do you need to replace the floor? Are there any cracks, holes or squeaks?

	Maintained	Repair
Floor condition is:	☐	☐
Wall condition is:	☐	☐
Ceiling condition is:	☐	☐
Artificial lighting is:	☐	☐

Is there a fire extinguisher? *(ABC type dry-chemical for all fires.)* Yes ☐ No ☐

Any daylight sunshine? *(Can you see without artificial lighting?)* Yes ☐ No ☐

Do the windows work properly? *(Is there any broken or cracked glass?)* Yes ☐ No ☐

Total windows in this area: One ☐ Two ☐ Three ☐ Four ☐ More_____ None ☐

Total windows, screens or storms: Damaged_____ Missing_____

Window treatments: Drapes ☐ Shutters ☐ Blinds ☐ Verticals ☐ None ☐

Total electric outlets are:_____ **Total heat or air registers in this area are:**_____

The total inches of insulation are: Walls_____ Ceiling_____ None ☐

Over-all Condition: Well-maintained ☐ Needs repair ☐

Note: Is there enough room for storing your lawn furniture, storm windows, snowmobiles, bicycles, motorcycles, riding mower, and do you have enough room for a work bench?

DETACHED GARAGE SERVICE DOOR

Construction is: Wood ☐ Steel ☐ Aluminum ☐ Other _____

Is there a window? *(Will the window open for ventilation?)*   Yes ☐ No ☐

Do the doors and lock(s) work properly?   Yes ☐ No ☐

Over-all Condition: Well-maintained ☐ Needs repair ☐

DETACHED GARAGE DOOR

Door dimensions: Height_____ Width_____

Construction is: Wood ☐ Steel ☐ Aluminum ☐ Vinyl ☐ Fiberglass ☐

Other_____

Door swing direction is: Overhead ☐ Side-hinged ☐ Other _____

Is there a weather strip attached to the bottom of the garage door to produce a weather-tight seal and keep animals out?   Yes ☐ No ☐

Will the garage door lock?   Yes ☐ No ☐

Any windows on the garage door? *(Is there any broken or cracked glass?)*   Yes ☐ No ☐

Is there an electric garage-door opener?   Yes ☐ No ☐

Do you have the door-opener remote controls?   Yes ☐ No ☐

The manufacturer's name is:_____

The style or type of door is:_____

Over-all Condition: Well-maintained ☐ Needs repair ☐

NOTE: Remember to take possession of the garage-door remote controls at the house closing.

Notes: _____

Notes:

---

*This space is for an area photograph, notes, drawings, or for listing the contents and features of this area, such as furniture, art, TV, stereo, location of skylights, etc. For a complete listing of home contents, use the **Home Furnishings List** in the **Forms** section at the back of the book.*

OUT BUILDING ROOF

DANGER: <u>Never climb on the roof.</u> <u>Leave this to the professionals.</u> You can inspect the roof from the ground if you stand back and look carefully. If you cannot see the roof's details very well, use a telescope or binoculars.

Construction is: Wood ☐   Asphalt ☐   Shingle ☐   Asbestos ☐   Cement ☐   Slate ☐   Tile ☐   Metal ☐   Other_____

Estimated age of roof in: Years_____   Months_____

Have you recently repaired the roof?   Yes ☐   No ☐

Is there roof ventilation? *(Keeps the attic cool and prolongs roof life.)*   Yes ☐   No ☐

Are there any tree limbs on the roof? *(Avoid roof damage.)*   Yes ☐   No ☐

Does the roof sag or bow? *(Roof may be weak. Contact a roofer.)*   Yes ☐   No ☐

Are there any roof leaks? *(Check inside ceilings for water leaks.)*   Yes ☐   No ☐

Flashing condition is: *(Prevents water leaks.)*   Maintained ☐   Repair ☐

Seals around vents are: *(Prevents water leaks.)*   Maintained ☐   Repair ☐

Over-all Condition: Well-maintained ☐   Needs repair ☐

Check here if the roof is snow covered and could not be examined. ☐

OUT BUILDING EXTERIOR

Dimensions: Length_____   Width_____   Height_____

Your lot survey can help you with precise home exterior & lot dimensions.

Construction is: Brick ☐   Aluminum ☐   Vinyl ☐   Wood ☐   Shingle ☐   Asbestos ☐   Block ☐   Stucco ☐   Stone ☐   Other_____

Paint and caulking is: Maintained ☐   Repair ☐

Gutters & downspouts are: Maintained ☐   Repair ☐

Total faucet bibs are:_____   **Total electrical outlets (GFCIs) are:**_____

Over-all Condition: Well-maintained ☐   Needs repair ☐

OUT BUILDING INTERIOR

Dimensions: Length_____ Width_____ Height_____

The floor is: Concrete ☐ Tile ☐ Brick ☐ Linoleum ☐ Asphalt ☐ Painted ☐
Other _____

The walls are: Plaster ☐ Drywall ☐ Wood ☐ Tile ☐ Wallpaper ☐ Unfinished ☐
Other _____

The ceiling is: Plaster ☐ Drywall ☐ Wood ☐ Tile ☐ Wallpaper ☐ Unfinished ☐
Other _____

Approximate Floor color is:_____

Wall color is:_____

Ceiling color is:_____

Do you need to replace the floor? Are there any cracks, holes or squeaks?

Floor condition is: Maintained ☐ Repair ☐
Wall condition is: Maintained ☐ Repair ☐
Ceiling condition is: Maintained ☐ Repair ☐
Artificial lighting is: Maintained ☐ Repair ☐

Is there a fire extinguisher? *(ABC type dry-chemical for all fires.)* Yes ☐ No ☐
Any daylight sunshine? *(Can you see without artificial lighting?)* Yes ☐ No ☐
Do the windows work properly? *(Is there any broken or cracked glass?)* Yes ☐ No ☐
Total windows in this area: One ☐ Two ☐ Three ☐ Four ☐ More_____ None ☐
Total windows, screens or storms: Damaged_____ Missing_____
Window treatments: Drapes ☐ Shutters ☐ Blinds ☐ Verticals ☐ None ☐
Total electric outlets are:_____ Total heat or air registers in this area are:_____
The total inches of insulation are: Walls_____ Ceiling_____ None ☐

Over-all Condition: Well-maintained ☐ Needs repair ☐

Note: Is there enough room for storing your lawn furniture, storm windows, snowmobiles, bicycles, motorcycles, riding mower, and do you have enough room for a work bench?

OUT BUILDING DRIVE & WALKWAY

Construction is: Brick ☐ Stone ☐ Concrete ☐ Asphalt ☐ Wood ☐
Other_____

Helpful Tip: The ground should angle downward from the house. Will the drive and walkway rain water drain away from the house?

Is there artificial lighting? *(Can you see the driveway at night?)* Yes ☐ No ☐

Over-all Condition: Well-maintained ☐ Needs repair ☐

Check here if this area is snow covered and could not be examined. ☐

OUT BUILDING SERVICE DOOR

Construction is: Wood ☐ Steel ☐ Aluminum ☐ Other_____

Is there a window? *(Will the window open for ventilation?)* Yes ☐ No ☐

Do the doors and lock(s) work properly? Yes ☐ No ☐

Over-all Condition: Well-maintained ☐ Needs repair ☐

OUT BUILDING GARAGE DOOR

Door dimensions: Height_____ Width_____

Construction is: Wood ☐ Steel ☐ Aluminum ☐ Vinyl ☐ Fiberglass ☐
Other_____

Door swing direction is: Overhead ☐ Side-hinged ☐ Other_____

Is there a weather strip attached to the bottom of the garage door to produce a weather-tight seal and keep animals out? Yes ☐ No ☐

Will the garage door lock? Yes ☐ No ☐

Any windows on the garage door? *(Is there any broken or cracked glass?)* Yes ☐ No ☐

Is there an electric garage-door opener? Yes ☐ No ☐

Do you have the door-opener remote controls? Yes ☐ No ☐

The manufacturer's name is:_____

The style or type of door is:_____

Over-all Condition: Well-maintained ☐ Needs repair ☐

NOTE: Remember to take possession of the garage-door remote controls at the house closing.

 **Notes:**

---

*This space is for an area photograph, notes, drawings, or for listing the contents and features of this area, such as furniture, art, TV, stereo, location of skylights, etc. For a complete listing of home contents, use the **Home Furnishings List** in the **Forms** section at the back of the book.*

SWIMMING POOL

The pool installation date was: Month _____ Day _____ Year _____

Type is: In Ground ☐   Above Ground ☐

Style is: Square ☐ Rectangular ☐ Round ☐ Oval ☐ Free form ☐
Other_____

Do you have the owner's manuals for the swimming pool and equipment? Yes ☐ No ☐

The pool manufacturer's name is:_____

Address:_____ **Phone:**_____

Service company:_____ **Phone:**_____

The pool's dimensions are: Width_____ Length_____

Helpful Tip: Use the information below to estimate your pool's average depth and gallon capacity. To estimate the water's depth in the shallow and deep ends of your pool, use your vacuum pole and a crayon. Enter the pool and lightly place the rubber-handled end of the pole on the pool floor. Mark the surface of the water with the crayon on the pole. Remove the pole from the swimming pool and measure the distance from the handle's end to the crayon mark using a tape measure.

Start Here   _____ + _____ = _____
                    Shallow-end depth   *Deep-end depth*   *Sub-total*

Divided by 2 = _____ X _____ X _____
                    Pool's average depth   *Width*   *Length*

Times   7.5 for Square & Rectangles = _____ Gallons
            6.7 for Oval & Freeform   Equals the total estimated
            5.9 for Round   gallon capacity

Note: If you have any difficulty estimating your pool's total gallon capacity or evaluating the over-all condition of the pool and its equipment, you may want to contact your local swimming pool supply company for assistance.

Construction is: Concrete ☐ Vinyl ☐ Fiberglass ☐ Metal ☐ Wood ☐
Other_____

The filter is: Sand ☐ Diatomaceous earth (D.E.) ☐ Paper cartridge ☐
Other_____

The filter size is:_____ **Amount of sand or D.E. used is:**_____

The pump motor size is:_____ hp. **Electric supply is:** 110 volts ☐ 220 volts ☐

Is the pump on an automatic timer? *(Saves electricity.)* Yes ☐ No ☐

Is there an automatic chlorination system? *(Controls chlorine usage.)* Yes ☐ No ☐

Is there an automatic pool cleaner? *(Pool is always ready for use.)* Yes ☐ No ☐

Is there a solar cover? *(The sun will heat your water free.)* Yes ☐ No ☐

Are there underwater pool lights? *(Where is the on/off switch?)* Yes ☐ No ☐

The electric supply for the pool light is: 110 volts ☐ 12 volts ☐

Is there a diving or jump board? *(Can be dangerous. Think safety.)* Yes ☐ No ☐

Are there any stairs, ladders or handrails installed? *(Think safety.)* Yes ☐ No ☐

Is the pool heated? *(Extends the swimming season.)* Yes ☐ No ☐

The heater uses: Electricity ☐ Natural gas ☐ Liquid propane (LP) gas ☐ Oil ☐
Solar ☐ Other_____

Is there artificial lighting? *(Can you see the pool at night?)* Yes ☐ No ☐

Over-all condition: Well maintained ☐ Needs repair ☐

Check here if this area is snow covered and could not be examined. ☐

Helpful Tip: Electricity and water do not mix. You must always have the correct grounding and use of GFCIs. Consult your local electrical inspector or electrician for more information.

Always consult with your local swimming-pool, whirlpool or hot-tub supply company. They can give you more information about water analysis, chemicals, equipment, filtration, and safety equipment.

*Notes:*_____

WHIRLPOOL OR HOT TUB

The pool installation date was: Month _____ Day _____ Year _____

Type is: In Ground ☐   Above Ground ☐

Style is: Square ☐   Rectangular ☐   Round ☐   Oval ☐   Free form ☐

Other _____

Do you have the owner's manuals for the pool and equipment?   Yes ☐   No ☐

The pool manufacturer's name is: _____

Address: _____ **Phone:** _____

Service company: _____ **Phone:** _____

The pool's dimensions are: Width _____   Length _____

Helpful Tip: Use the information below to estimate your pool's average depth and gallon capacity. To estimate the water's depth in the shallow and deep ends of your pool, use your vacuum pole and a crayon. Enter the pool and lightly place the rubber-handled end of the pole on the pool floor. Mark the surface of the water with the crayon on the pole. Remove the pole from the swimming pool and measure the distance from the handle's end to the crayon mark using a tape measure.

Start Here   _____ + _____ = _____
                 Shallow-end depth   Deep-end depth   Sub-total

Divided by 2 =   _____ X _____ X _____
                     Pool's average depth   Width   Length

Times   7.5 for Square & Rectangles = _____ Gallons
            6.7 for Oval & Freeform   Equals the total estimated
            5.9 for Round   gallon capacity

Note: If you have any difficulty estimating your pool's total gallon capacity or evaluating the over-all condition of the pool and its equipment, you may want to contact your local swimming pool/hot tub supply company for assistance.

Construction is: Concrete ☐ Vinyl ☐ Fiberglass ☐ Metal ☐ Wood ☐
Other_____

The filter is: Sand ☐ Diatomaceous earth (D.E.) ☐ Paper cartridge ☐
Other_____

The filter size is:_____ **Amount of sand or D.E. used is:**_____

The pump motor size is:_____h.p. **Electric supply is:** 110 volts ☐ 220 volts ☐

Blower size is:_____h.p. **Electric** ☐ **No blower - air induction** ☐
(Forced air) *(A tube type siphon)*

Is the pump on an automatic timer? *(Saves electricity.)* Yes ☐ No ☐

Are there underwater pool lights? *(Where is the on/off switch?)* Yes ☐ No ☐

The electric supply for the pool light is: 110 volts ☐ 12 volts ☐

Is there an automatic chemical feed? *(Bacteria control is important.)* Yes ☐ No ☐

Is there an ozonator? *(Electronic bacteria control.)* Yes ☐ No ☐

Is there an insulating cover? *(Will the cover snap or lock tight?)* Yes ☐ No ☐

Are there any stairs, ladders or handrails installed? *(Think safety.)* Yes ☐ No ☐

The heater uses: Electricity ☐ Natural gas ☐ Liquid propane (LP) gas ☐ Oil ☐
Solar ☐ Other_____

Is there artificial lighting? *(Can you see the pool at night?)* Yes ☐ No ☐

Over-all condition: Well maintained ☐ Needs repair ☐

Check here if this area is snow covered and could not be examined. ☐

Helpful Tip: Electricity and water do not mix. You must always have the correct grounding and use of GFCIs. Consult your local electrical inspector or electrician for more information.

Always consult with your local swimming-pool, whirlpool or hot-tub supply company. They can give you more information about water analysis, chemicals, equipment, filtration, and safety equipment.

Notes:_____

POOL PATIO

Patio dimensions: Length _____ Width _____

Construction is: Concrete ☐ Wood ☐ Brick ☐ Stone ☐
Cool Decking ☐ Aluminum ☐ Outdoor Carpet ☐
Other _____

Pool area fencing is: Concrete ☐ Wood ☐ Metal ☐ Cyclone ☐
Other _____

The fence height is: _____ Feet, and _____ Inches

Is the pool deck in good condition? *(Are there any major problems?)*   Yes ☐   No ☐

Is this area screen enclosed? *(Are mosquitoes a problem?)*   Yes ☐   No ☐

Are there any holes in the screen?   Yes ☐   No ☐

Do the gate(s) and/or door(s) work and lock properly?   Yes ☐   No ☐

Are the outlets on GFCIs? *(Safety device for wet locations.)*   Yes ☐   No ☐

Is there artificial lighting? *(Can you see the pool at night?)*   Yes ☐   No ☐

Over-all condition: Well-maintained ☐   Needs repair ☐

Check here if this area is snow covered and cannot be examined. ☐

BARBECUE

Will the barbecue remain?   Yes ☐   No ☐

The barbecue is: Permanent ☐   Portable ☐

Construction is: Brick ☐ Stone ☐ Metal ☐ Concrete ☐
Other _____

The fuel supply is: Natural Gas ☐ Liquid Propane (LP gas) ☐ Charcoal ☐
Wood ☐ Other _____

Is there a work counter attached?   Yes ☐   No ☐

Over-all condition: Well-maintained ☐   or Needs Repair ☐

Notes:

*This space is for an area photograph, notes, drawings, or for listing the contents and features of this area, such as furniture, art, TV, stereo, location of skylights, etc. For a complete listing of home contents, use the **Home Furnishings List** in the **Forms** section at the back of the book.*

Notes:

This space is for an area photograph, notes, drawings, or for listing the contents and features of this area, such as furniture, art, TV, stereo, location of skylights, etc. For a complete listing of home contents, use the **Home Furnishings List** *in the* **Forms** *section at the back of the book.*

GLOSSARY

Access Door:	A loose panel overhead in hall or bedroom for easy access to the attic.
Amperage:	A measurement of electricity.
Asbestos:	It was used to insulate pipe, exterior walls and in roofing materials. If asbestos deteriorates, it can pose a serious threat of lung cancer. It is costly to replace and dispose of.
Chimney Flue:	A pipe or chamber for elimination of gasses of fumes.
Circuit Breaker:	A switch that automatically stops the flow of electric current in an overloaded circuit.
Caulking:	Used to seal any joints or cracks to prevent penetration of moisture.
Damper:	In a fireplace, an adjustable plate to control the passage of heat.
Downspout:	Vertical pipes from the gutters of a roof to the ground.
Drywall:	A pre-cast interior wallboard. Also know as "gypsum board" or "sheetrock."
Eaves:	The under part of a roof that extends beyond the wall.
Electric Outlet:	A receptacle that has a socket for a plug and is connected to a power supply.
Faucet Bib:	Also called a "hose bib" or a "Water spigot." It connects to a garden hose.
Flashing:	Sheet metal or tar paper used at different points in a structure to prevent water leakage such as around roofs, vent pipes, chimneys, or windows.
Fuse:	An electrical safety device that melts when the circuit is overloaded.
GFCI:	**Ground Fault Circuit Interrupter** - Measures for electric current leakage. It is also a safety device that interrupts an electric circuit when the currents are not equal.

Ground:	To connect an electric current to the ground.
Gutters:	A channel along the eaves that directs rain water to a downspout.
Hearth Extension:	The stone or brick floor immediately in front of the fireplace.
Insulation:	This is a material that is placed in structures to reduce the rate of heat loss or gain. It can also help to reduce a fire hazard.
Lead-Base Paint:	Found in older homes, it can be very hazardous to small children. Very costly to remove, and was banned in 1970.
Lumber Dry Rot:	A fungus disease of timber that causes it to become brittle and to crumble.
Mortar:	A mix of cement with sand and water, used in masonry to bond blocks, bricks and stones together.
Out Building:	A building, like a shed or barn, separate from the main building.
Radon Gas:	Odorless, colorless gas that is released naturally wherever uranium is present in the soil.
R-Value:	Also knows as "R-Factor" & "R-Rating." A figure used to show the insulating value per inch of a product. The higher the R-Value, the more effective the insulation.
Septic Tank:	A Tank in which sewage is decomposed by bacteria when city sewers are not available.
Termites:	Termites are highly destructive insects that usually feed on wood.
Thermostat:	A mechanism that controls the heat or air-conditioning temperature automatically.
Urea Formaldehyde:	A thick (1-1/2 inch) white insulation. If not installed properly, it can be a health threat. The removal is messy, difficult, and very costly.
Voltage:	A measurement of the intensity of electricity.

REAL ESTATE TERMINOLOGY

These are a few of the more common terms you may hear in discussions surrounding the purchase or sale of a home. There are many others, but these will be used most often.

Abstract of Title: History of property. A summary of all matters and legal proceedings showing owner names, land descriptions, agreements, etc.

Appraisal: An estimate of the market value of property.

Appreciation: An increase in the value of your property due to economic changes.

Assessed Valuation: A percentage of appraised value for tax purposes. The value of real estate set by the county assessor for the purpose of assessing taxes.

Assuming a Mortgage: An act by the buyer whereby he/she assumes the former owner's obligations to repay the loan or mortgage.

Binder: A document that sets forth the contractual understanding between the buyer and the seller. Sometimes referred to as an "earnest money receipt."

Closing: At this transaction, the buyer receives ownership of the property and the seller receives his moneys.

Closing Statement: A statement to the buyer and the seller that informs each party regarding the receipt and disbursement of all funds.

Closing Points: These are the fees charged by the lending institution for processing and handling the loan. Each point is equal to one percent of the amount being loaned.

Compound Interest: Interest paid both on the original principal and interest previously earned.

Contingency: Dependent on a condition. *Example:* "This agreement is contingent upon all major repairs being completed before closing on the house."

Contract: An agreement between two parties whereby each of the parties makes certain pledges. The seller to give title and possession and the buyer to pay a particular price.

Deed: A legal document stating ownership of real property.

Deposit: This is "Earnest Moneys" given by the buyer to show evidence or good faith in his/her contractual obligation to buy real property.

Deed Restricted:	Any stipulation in a deed restricting ownership or use of property.
Easement:	The legal right to use another person's property for restricted purposes.
Equity:	The value of your home over and above the amount of the mortgage balance.
Escrow Holder:	A third party entrusted by both buyer and seller to handle specific details of the transaction.
Interest:	The cost of borrowing money.
First Mortgage:	A mortgage that has priority over all other mortgages.
G.I. Loan (VA):	A loan that is guaranteed by the Veterans' Administration.
Joint Tenancy:	Ownership of property shared by two or more persons, including a right of survivorship.
Legal Description:	A description that legally describes the real property according to a lot survey or map.
Lien:	Any legal claim against a property to satisfy an obligation or debt.
Market Value:	The price a buyer is willing to pay and the seller is willing to receive, not necessarily based on replacement cost or relative value.
Mortgage:	A legal instrument where the owner of property pledges it as security to guarantee repayment of a loan.
Principal:	The original amount that is borrowed.
Quit-Claim Deed:	A deed that conveys whatever interest a seller may have in the property.
Survey:	Will show the legal boundaries of the property and the location of the house and any other buildings that might be on the lot.
Title:	A legal document of ownership.
Title Insurance:	Property insurance to protect the owner against any other claims of ownership. A one-time cost at the time of purchase. Title insurance lasts as long as you own the property.
Warranty Deed:	A deed whereby the seller guarantees that the title is good.

Records
And
Forms

Notes:

SUMMARY OF ESTIMATES

For easy calculations we have compiled this list for your estimated maintenance or repair costs. We have listed the appropriate page numbers on the left-hand side. Fill in the blanks as necessary to arrive at your total estimate for each specified area. This can be helpful to justify your improvement or repair expenses when selling your home.

Page Number	Description	Totals
11	Yard & Landscape	$ _____
11	Exterior Roof	_____
12	Home Exterior	_____
13	Front Entrance	_____
13	Back Entrance	_____
13	Side Entrance	_____
15	Awnings or Shutters	_____
15	Windows and Doors	_____
16	Outdoor Patio	_____
16	Drive & Walkway	_____
17	Attic Area	_____
18	Insulation	_____
20	Water System	_____
21	Water Heater	_____
21	Water Treatment	_____
22	City Sewage System	_____
22	Septic Tank System	_____
23	Electrical System	_____
25	Heating System	_____

SUB-TOTAL PAGE # 89 $ _____

SUMMARY OF ESTIMATES

Page Number	Description	Totals
25	Air Conditioning System	$ _____
27	Foyer & Vestibule	_____
28	Kitchen	_____
30	Kitchen Appliances	_____
32	Dining Room	_____
34	Formal Dining Room	_____
36	Living Room	_____
38	Family Room	_____
40	Library or Den	_____
42	Lanai or Enclosed Porch	_____
44	Master Bedroom	_____
46	Bedroom Number Two	_____
48	Bedroom Number Three	_____
50	Bedroom Number Four	_____
52	Master Bathroom	_____
54	Bathroom Number Two	_____
56	Bathroom Number Three	_____
58	Hallway	_____
59	Stairway	_____
60	Basement	_____
62	Laundry Room	_____
65	Attached Garage Interior	_____

SUB-TOTAL PAGE # 90 $ _____

SUMMARY OF ESTIMATES

Page Number	Description	Totals
66	Attached Garage Service Door	$ _____
66	Attached Garage Door	_____
68	Detached Garage Roof	_____
68	Detached Garage Exterior	_____
69	Detached Garage Interior	_____
70	Detached Garage Service Door	_____
70	Detached Garage Door	_____
72	Out Building Roof	_____
72	Out Building Exterior	_____
73	Out Building Interior	_____
74	Out Building Drive & Walkway	_____
74	Out Building Service Door	_____
74	Out Building Garage Door	_____
76	Swimming Pool	_____
78	Whirlpool or Hot Tub	_____
80	Pool Patio	_____
80	Barbecue	_____

SUB-TOTAL PAGE # 89 $ _____

SUB-TOTAL PAGE # 90 $ _____

SUB-TOTAL PAGE # 91 $ _____

TOTAL OF ALL PAGES $ _____

HOME IMPROVEMENT PRIORITY LIST

Use this list to keep your priorities on target. Record the problem, solutions, cost, and the estimated time in months. As a buyer, seller or current home owner you can pinpoint existing problems and accurately justify these expenses to fulfill your short, midway or long-term goals.

Problem	Solution	Cost	1-6 mo.	7-12 mo.	13-24 mo.
_____	_____	_____	☐	☐	☐
_____	_____	_____	☐	☐	☐
_____	_____	_____	☐	☐	☐
_____	_____	_____	☐	☐	☐
_____	_____	_____	☐	☐	☐
_____	_____	_____	☐	☐	☐
_____	_____	_____	☐	☐	☐
_____	_____	_____	☐	☐	☐
_____	_____	_____	☐	☐	☐
_____	_____	_____	☐	☐	☐
_____	_____	_____	☐	☐	☐
_____	_____	_____	☐	☐	☐
_____	_____	_____	☐	☐	☐
_____	_____	_____	☐	☐	☐
_____	_____	_____	☐	☐	☐
_____	_____	_____	☐	☐	☐
_____	_____	_____	☐	☐	☐
_____	_____	_____	☐	☐	☐
_____	_____	_____	☐	☐	☐
_____	_____	_____	☐	☐	☐
_____	_____	_____	☐	☐	☐
_____	_____	_____	☐	☐	☐
_____	_____	_____	☐	☐	☐
_____	_____	_____	☐	☐	☐
_____	_____	_____	☐	☐	☐
_____	_____	_____	☐	☐	☐
_____	_____	_____	☐	☐	☐
_____	_____	_____	☐	☐	☐
_____	_____	_____	☐	☐	☐
_____	_____	_____	☐	☐	☐
_____	_____	_____	☐	☐	☐
_____	_____	_____	☐	☐	☐

REPAIR AND IMPROVEMENT SUMMARY

We provided this summary to help you record your house expenses. Enter each expense at the time of purchase and save all bills in a large manila envelope. This important information can save you thousands of dollars in possible tax benefits when selling your home, or assist you if a necessary insurance claim arises.

Home Repairs or Improvements	Date	Repair Cost	Improvement Cost
		$	$

Sub Total $ _____ $ _____

Home Repairs or Improvements	Date	Repair Cost	Improvement Cost
		$	$

Total Home Repairs or Improvements $ _____ $ _____

Notes:

Use this space for notes, additional comments, and/or recording items not listed on the other side of this form.

Notes:

Use this space for notes, additional comments, and/or recording items not listed on the other side of this form.

HOME INFORMATION FORM FOR BUYERS & SELLERS

Provided By George M. Johnson

Owner's Name: _____
Address: _____
City: _____
State & Zip: _____
County: _____

Folio Number: _____
Sale or Purchase price of home: $_____
Total square footage is: _____
Lot size is: _____ x _____
Last year's property tax bill was: $_____

Year built and purchased: _____ _____
Home's construction is: _____
Home style or design is: _____
Siding material is: _____
Roofing material is: _____

Builder's name (if known): _____
Number of bedrooms: _____
Number of bathrooms: _____
Total number of actual rooms: _____
Number of closets: _____

Monthly Expenses are:
Fuel .... $_____
Electric .... $_____
Water .... $_____
Trash pick-up .... $_____
    Monthly Total $_____

Trash pick-up: City ☐   Private ☐
Public transportation: Yes ☐   No ☐
Schools: Grade ☐   Junior ☐   High ☐   High ☐   Parochial ☐

Home's heat & air-conditioning fuel is:
 Electric ☐   Gas ☐   Oil ☐   Coal ☐   Solar ☐   Wood ☐
Electric service is:
 60 amp ☐   100 amp ☐   200 amp ☐   400 amp ☐
Water source is
 City ☐   Well ☐   Private ☐   Community ☐
Sewer system is: City ☐   Septic Tank ☐
Septic Tank gallon capacity is: _____
Pool/Hot tub heating fuel is: _____

ROOMS	DIMENSIONS	FLOOR & WALL COVERING	FEATURES		
Living	___ x ___	_____	Central air	Yes ☐	No ☐
Dinette	___ x ___	_____	Dishwasher	Yes ☐	No ☐
Formal Dining	___ x ___	_____	Disposal	Yes ☐	No ☐
Kitchen	___ x ___	_____	Oven/Range	Yes ☐	No ☐
Family	___ x ___	_____	Stove	Yes ☐	No ☐
Laundry	___ x ___	_____	Trash Compactor	Yes ☐	No ☐
Den	___ x ___	_____	Refrigerator	Yes ☐	No ☐
Bathroom #1	___ x ___	_____	Humidifier	Yes ☐	No ☐
Bathroom #2	___ x ___	_____	Patio	Yes ☐	No ☐
Bathroom #3	___ x ___	_____	Screened Porch	Yes ☐	No ☐
Bedroom #1	___ x ___	_____	Fireplace(s)	Yes ☐	No ☐
Bedroom #2	___ x ___	_____	Drapes/Blinds	Yes ☐	No ☐
Bedroom #3	___ x ___	_____	Garage	Yes ☐	No ☐
Bedroom #4	___ x ___	_____	Pool	Yes ☐	No ☐
Bedroom #5	___ x ___	_____	Hot tub	Yes ☐	No ☐

Basement is: Full ☐   Partial ☐   None ☐   Water Heater   Gas ☐   Elect. ☐
Foundation is: Block ☐   Poured concrete ☐   Other_____   Gallon capacity _____
                                    Water Purification System
The home's over-all condition is: Maintained ☐   Needs repair ☐   Owned ☐   Rented ☐   None ☐

OTHER FEATURES _____
_____

COMMENTS _____
_____
_____
_____
_____

Notes:

Use this space for notes, additional comments, and/or recording items not listed on the other side of this form.

HOME FURNISHINGS LIST

Keep an accurate and up-to-date list of the contents of your home, such as furniture, art, TV, stereo, jewelry, power tools, etc. You may want to take photographs or a video tape of these items for proof if an insurance claim arises.

Manufacturer's Name	Model	Purchase Date	Cost

HOME FURNISHINGS LIST

Manufacturer's Name	Model	Purchase Date	Cost

Seasonal Check List

Use this list to maintain an up-to-date record of your home's important seasonal preparations. For example: when to drain the outside water faucets, store garden hoses or tune up the snow blower. This information can be very helpful to another person if you are not available to do it yourself.

WINTER

SPRING

SUMMER

FALL

MAINTENANCE SCHEDULE

Provided By

Technihouse Inspections inc.
Residential & Commercial Inspection Company
4940 Rands Road / Bloomfield Hills, MI 48302
(810) 855-5566

Also available from Technihouse
- Environmental Inspections
- Structural and mechanical components analyses
- Licensed pest inspections
- New construction inspections
- Remodeling consultations and structural recommendations.

	ONCE/INITIALLY	PERIODICALLY	SPRING/SUMMER	FALL	ANNUALLY
I EXTERIOR: Roof and gutters					
a. Check for damaged, loose or missing shingles.			✓	✓	
b. Examine the chimney flashing to assure against leaks (the flashing is the metal that prevents leakage around chimney and walls where they meet roofing shingles).			✓	✓	
c. Examine the flashing around skylights and room stacks to make sure there are no cracks or gaps.			✓	✓	
d. Cut back any tree branches or limbs hanging within two to three feet of your roof. The weight of snow and ice will drag them down and damage your shingles. Remove or cut back branches of trees and ivy from top of chimney.				✓	
e. Secure any loose antenna supports. Where they are attached to the roof examine area carefully for cracks or possible source of leakage.		✓			
f. Examine and repair all roof vents for broken, missing or obstructed screening; remove bird's nests.					✓
g. Install hardware cloth screen on chimney flues to keep birds, squirrels and raccoons out of the house.					✓
h. Examine chimney for any loose or missing bricks and tuck-point using ready-mix mortar if needed.				✓	
i. Clean gutters.		✓			
j. Secure loose gutters.			✓	✓	
k. Repair leaking gutter seams.				✓	
l. Install soffit vents under overhang to help eliminate winter ice dam problems (soffit vents are screens or plugs that go under the overhang and allow air to circulate above the insulation, through the attic, keeping roof surface colder.	✓				
II EXTERIOR: Walls					
a. Check for peeling paint; touch up as needed.					✓
b. Repair/replace damaged, loose, warped or deteriorating siding & trim.					✓
c. Examine masonry walls for cracked. loose or missing mortar and tuck-point using ready-mix mortar.			✓		
d. Slope the terrain away from the structure for at least four to six feet with at least a one-inch-per-foot slope. This will reduce moisture accumulation against foundation walls and help make the basement dryer in the spring.		✓			
e. Install plastic bubbles or covers over basement window wells to keep out leaves, rain and snow.	✓				
f. Caulk around all windows and trim and wherever two different materials meet (i.e. siding meets brick, aluminum abuts wood, etc.)		✓			
g. Caulk around all faucet bibs, outlets, lights, dryer vents, utility entrances, etc. (If you total up all the areas that need caulking around the average home, it would be equal to a three-foot hole in a wall or about the same as leaving a window open all winter.)		✓			
h. Examine and re-putty any loose, cracked or missing glazing compound around window glass.			✓		
i. Examine all doors for tightness and install weather-stripping if needed.			✓		
j. Remove window screens and store off the ground; repair/replace any damaged or torn screens or frames.				✓	
k. Clean windows and install storms.				✓	
l. Replace all cracked or broken window panes.			✓		
m. Install storm windows or plastic on the basement windows (Remember, that thin pane of glass is the only thing that separates you from a 60-degree temperature difference.)				✓	
n. Install window screens.			✓		
III EXTERIOR: Miscellaneous					
a. Replace all burned-out bulbs on porch, post and flood lights.		✓			
b. Stack firewood off the ground or it will deteriorate. It will also harbor mice and rodents.					✓
c. Turn off and drain all outside hose bibs, sprinklers and pool equipment.				✓	
d. Clean cracks in driveways and walkaways and fill with mortar, caulk, latex concrete patch or any viscous sealant to prevent moisture from entering the cracks, freezing and heaving or eroding the concrete or asphalt.					✓
e. Do not cover your air conditioning compressor. (Although experts differ, it is generally accepted that the compressor unit is designed to be outdoors; covering it could accelerate rust and corrosion while providing a home for field mice or chipmunks who cannot forage food in severe weather and will start nibbling on the wire's insulation.)				✓	
IV Miscellaneous equipment					
a. Check the oil in your snowblower; it's probably a good idea to replace it with fresh 5-W-30 oil, which is a good winter oil that makes the engine easier to start.				✓	
b. Check oil & gas, change spark plug. Sharpen Blade on Lawnmower.			✓		
c. If you left fuel in the tank from last winter/summer and did not add Sta-bil, a gasoline additive that keeps stored gas fresh, then drain and add fresh gasoline.					✓
d. Replace snowblower spark plug.				✓	
e. Check grease in the gear box on the auger of the blower.				✓	
f. Start the blower's engine to make sure it will start when there is snow on the ground.				✓	

Because of the general nature of this advice and the individual application thereof, neither the *American Society of Home Inspectors* or *Technihouse Inspections, Inc.* assume any responsibility for any loss, cost, damage, injury or expense which may be incurred or suffered as a result of the use of this material.

Task	Once/Initially	Periodically	Spring/Summer	Fall	Annually
g. Tighten loose handles or grips on your shovels.					√
h. Sand and paint rusting metal sections; pound out and straighten bent corners.					√
i. Buy rock salt or de-icing compound early while it's on sale; store in a convenient and accessible place.					√
j. Store hoses, rakes, brooms, edgers, etc., for the winter.				√	
k. Cordless electric equipment such as edgers and trimmers should be run down to almost the end of the battery life and brought indoors for the winter. Don't keep the battery pack on a charger all winter. Just recharge before you use it again in spring.				√	
l. Fill lawn mower with gas and add a couple of drops of Sta-bil (about $2 to $3 for a four-ounce can at lawn and garden suppliers) because gas gums up the carburetor as it evaporates and, if left empty, condensation could rust the interior.				√	
m. Store lawn mower in a cold place -- but not uncovered outside.				√	
n. Do not store lawn mower in the basement. Even if you decide to drain the gasoline tank, gas fumes present a hazard.					√
o. Check oil and fill if needed before storing. That way, condensation can't collect in that chamber.					√
p. Remove blade and sharpen.					√
q. Wash air filter using soap and water, then add 10 to 12 drops of oil to the sponge filter and squeeze it to evenly distribute the oil.					√
V Fireplace					
a. Look up, with caution, to check for loose bricks and obstructions. Remove whatever you see.		√			
b. If chimney flue has not been cleaned recently and you use the fireplace weekly, have it cleaned to prevent a chimney fire.					√
c. Examine fire box for loose or crumbling brick. Make necessary repairs using fire clay.		√			
d. Install glass fireplace doors to conserve energy and money.	√				
VI Crawl space					
a. Close all vents.				√	
b. If you have little or no insulation, add R-19 insulation to perimeter walls.	√				
c. A vapor barrier (generally four to six mil plastic) should be on the dirt ground of the crawl space.	√				
d. Insulate all plumbing pipes with wrap insulation.	√				
e. Open vents.			√		
VII Attic					
a. For severe winters, R-38 insulation is ideal. After R-19, your payback decreases dramatically. But if you're planning to live in your house quite awhile, install additional insulation.	√				
b. Do not close or obstruct attic vent openings. They should remain open to remove heat in summer and to help eliminate ice dams in winter.				√	
c. If your house has a whole house fan in the hall ceiling, install a plastic vapor barrier on top of it and then cover it with insulation to prevent heat loss.				√	
d. If your attic has any duct work make sure ducts are thoroughly insulated.	√				
VIII Windows					
a. Feel around all windows for possible drafts. If windows vibrate or are loose, tighten or secure them. If you have to, remove the window stop and reinstall it closer to the window sash, thus tightening loose windows. Keep in mind that doing this will probably disturb the painted finish along the window trip and jamb.				√	
b. Install inside storm windows around most of the older aluminum and steel windows.				√	
c. Paint as needed.		√			
IX Electrical					
a. Learn the location of main electrical disconnects, fuses or circuit breakers.		√			
b. Buy spare fuses. Generally, you should use only 20-amp fuses for the kitchen and laundry circuits and 15-amp fuses only for lighting and outlets. Never install oversized fuses.		√			
c. If you have Ground Fault Circuit Interrupters, trip and rest them monthly.		√			
d. Circuit breakers should be tripped and reset every six months to clean the contacts so they don't oxidize and become useless.			√	√	
e. Label each circuit.	√				
f. Visually inspect each lamp, extension and appliance cord and plug in the house. Immediately replace any that are frayed or broken.					√

	ONCE/INITIALLY	PERIODICALLY	SPRING/SUMMER	FALL	ANNUALLY
X Plumbing					
a. Know the location of the main water shut-off (near the water meter).	✓				
b. Know the location of the main HOT water shut-off (usually above or near the hot water tank)	✓				
c. Replace all worn or dripping faucet washer.		✓			
d. Drain exterior hose bibbs, water lines, sprinklers or pool equipment and any plumbing exposed to unheated areas.				✓	
e. Turn on all exterior hose bibbs.			✓		
XI Heating system					
a. Know the location of heating system service safety switch (usually on the side or above the heating system).	✓				
b. Remove all combustibles from anywhere near the furnace or hot water tank.		✓			
c. Oil the furnace or boiler motor or circulating pump (usually a 20- weight oil is best unless otherwise stated).			✓	✓	
d. Depress the fan belt in the middle. If it depresses more than an inch, it should be adjusted by loosening the motor mounts, pulling taut and re-tightening.					✓
e. Change the air filters or wash the electronic air filter.		✓			
f. Turn on water supply to the humidifier.				✓	
g. Turn off water supply & clean humidifier.			✓		
h. Watch the burner flame for a couple of minutes. It should burn a nice blue flame with a few orange or yellow areas. If it burns predominately yellow or orange, the gas/air mixture should be adjusted.				✓	
i. Have your furnace heat exchanger inspected by a licensed heating contractor or the gas company. The heat exchanger is the interior part of the furnace that separates carbon monoxide from the air you breathe. It should be inspected annually. If the inspector tells you it is cracked or corroded, get a second opinion since it usually means you'll have to replace the furnace.					✓
j. Lightly blow-off or dust your thermostat.					✓
k. On steam systems, every week blow-off or drain the low-water cut-off to prevent deposits from clogging the valve.		✓			
XII INTERIOR MISC.					
a. Repair/replace loose damaged floor coverings.		✓			
b. Caulk around bath tubs.		✓			
c. Grout tile in bathrooms.		✓			
d. Repair/replace loose/damaged ceramic tiles.		✓			
e. Tighten/repair cabinet & door hardware as well as hinges.		✓			
f. Install exhaust fans (vented & exterior) in bathrooms & kitchen.	✓				
g. Secure loose handrails & banisters.		✓			
h. Install smoke detectors.	✓				
i. Change batteries in smoke detectors.					✓
j. Clean/test smoke detectors.		✓			
k. Install fire extinguishers.	✓				
l. Clean refrigerator coil.		✓			
m. Check & repair/replace refrigerator gaskets as needed.					✓
n. Eliminate extension-cord wiring.					✓
o. Install ground fault circuit interrupters in kitchen, bathrooms & garage.	✓				

XIII PLANNING AHEAD

Will save you money, inconvenience -- and possibly your life. Not only should you plan for the normal seasonal conditions, but also those unforeseen. Keep emergency supplies on hand, including:

1. Flashlights with extra fresh batteries. 2. Extra blankets. 3. Candles and/or lantern. 4. Transistor radio with fresh batteries. 5. Canned foods with hand-operated can opener. 6. Kerosene heater with fresh kerosene. 7. Extra firewood if you have a fireplace.

MISC. _____

©1993 Technihouse Inspections, Incorporated
Member American Society of Home Inspectors